Where to Put Your
Money ***Now***

Where to Put Your
Money *Now*

How to Make Super-Safe Investments and Secure Your Future

PETER PASSELL

Pocket Books
New York   London   Toronto   Sydney

This publication contains the opinions and ideas of its author. It is sold with the understanding that neither the author nor the publisher is engaged in rendering legal, tax, investment, insurance, financial, accounting, or other professional advice or services. If the reader requires such advice or services, a competent professional should be consulted. Relevant laws vary from state to state. The strategies outlined in this book may not be suitable for every individual, and are not guaranteed or warranted to produce any particular results.

No warranty is made with respect to the accuracy or completeness of the information contained herein, and both the author and the publisher specifically disclaim any responsibility for any liability, loss, or risk, personal or otherwise, which is incurred as a consequence, directly or indirectly, of the use and application of any of the contents of this book.

 Pocket Books
A Division of Simon & Schuster, Inc.
1230 Avenue of the Americas
New York, NY 10020

The views expressed are those of the author and not necessarily those of the Milken Institute.

First Pocket Books trade edition February 2009.

POCKET and colophon are registered trademarks of Simon & Schuster, Inc.

For information about special discounts for bulk purchases, please contact Simon & Schuster Special Sales at 1-800-456-6798 or business@simonand-schuster.com

Designed by Elliott Beard

Manufactured in the United States of America

10 9 8 7 6 5 4 3 2 1

Library of Congress Cataloging-in-Publication Data

Passell, Peter.
   Where to put your money now : how to make super-safe investments and secure your future / Peter Passell.
      p. cm.
   1. Investments. 2. Finance, Personal. I. Title.
   HG4521.P363 2009
      332.6—dc22   2008048421

ISBN-13:   978-1-4391-4705-4
ISBN-10:   1-4391-4705-1

Contents

Introduction

What a difference a bubble can make. As recently as the spring of 2007, those nice folks in charge of Wall Street—the ones with $350 haircuts—were convinced they were the Masters of the Universe. Dozens of investment firms, some dating from the nineteenth century, were largely ignoring their traditional businesses, preferring instead to sell whiz-bang financial products cooked up by computer geeks. And why not? You didn't have to burn the midnight oil for those profits—they just poured in!

Regulators sometimes frowned at the pace and complexity of the new business, one in which the dizzying electronic shuffle of complex financial contracts had largely replaced the more familiar task of issuing and trading stocks and bonds. But in an era in which the financial services industry was growing faster than any other in America and foreigners were paying homage by trusting Wall Street with trillions of their dollars, the underpaid lawyers in charge of securities law enforcement largely lacked the stomach to challenge the new practices.

Besides, Main Street got to go along for the ride. A select few were given the opportunity to entrust their savings to the self-described wizards who ran unregulated "hedge funds" and watched the triple-digit returns—that's right, 100 percent returns—roll in. Far more important, millions of middle-income Americans benefited indirectly, gaining unprecedented access to capital. Not so long ago, after all, banks were famous for lending only to people who didn't need the money. Now they were tripping over each other to provide cash to any warm body inclined to buy a house.

The housing market, of course, was ground zero for the financing revolution. Can't afford a down payment? You won't need one if you're willing to shell out a little more interest. Can't afford the monthly payments? We'll lend you the money anyway, as long as you just pretend you can pay. Hoping to get a better job next year? We'll give you a "teaser rate" that won't ratchet up to market-rate interest for three years. And if you still can't pay full freight in three years, we'll be happy to refinance your mortgage after the house goes up in value.

Some of the people who couldn't resist the pitches of the what-me-worry? mortgage brokers were the same sort who considered the Powerball lottery a prudent investment. But many were simply folks with modest incomes who never thought they could afford to buy a house within commuting distance of Los Angeles or Seattle or Miami, and were thrilled to be told otherwise.

Then, in the spring of 2006, the housing bubble began to leak. House prices had fallen before, and the world had pretty much stayed the same. But this time around, one financial institution after another teetered and fell in spite of the hesitant efforts of the federal government to contain the damage.

By late in the summer of 2008, the nation's financial markets were in gridlock.

As these words were being written, Washington was throwing money—a sum that could easily exceed $1 *trillion*—at the problem. And the best guess now is that almost unlimited cash and the political will to spend it on the bailout will prove sufficient to turn the corner. But that's hardly the end of the story. Investors, especially the ones like you and me who lack golden parachutes or wads of hundred-dollar bills stashed in Swiss bank vaults, would be foolish to ignore the evidence that the safest of financial systems in the richest nation on earth can go south in a hurry. So all of us would do well to rethink the way we invest the savings needed for retirement or college bills—or, yes, even houses.

The first chapter of the book offers a bite-size explanation for the meltdown. No heavy lifting; no pop quiz at the end. However, if you'd like to cut to the chase, be my guest. Skip the analysis of what went wrong and go directly to chapter 2, where I lay out the broad implications of the panic for investors.

Or, if you're really in a hurry, you can move right on to the practical advice in the rest of the book. Chapter 3 spells out the options for bulletproofing your savings, focusing on investments that eliminate all but the most remote chance of losing money. Chapter 4 offers choices for investors who are still prepared to accept some risk in return for a fighting chance to earn higher returns.

After sifting through the possible investments, of course, you'll still need to decide on the right box to put them in. Chapter 5 describes the pros and cons of the myriad ways to take advantage of Uncle Sam's desire that you save more for education or retirement.

While the advice in this book is up-to-the-minute as of publication, some of it has a short shelf life. So in chapter 6, I offer a short tour of Web sites that provide timely information—most of it for free.

Happy hunting.

ONE

What Went Wrong

Back when Americans listened to music recorded on vinyl and cars had tail fins, buying a house was straightforward—if not always easy. First you saved for a down payment, then went to a local bank or savings and loan to apply for a mortgage. The bank checked your income and credit records, verified that the down payment was ample to protect its investment in the unlikely event of a foreclosure, and provided the necessary cash from the savings deposits entrusted to it by your neighbors. What you saw was what you got: a mortgage with a fixed monthly payment that would be paid off twenty years down the road.

But big changes were coming—most of them built around the entry of Wall Street into the home mortgage market. Actually, the seeds of these changes had been planted decades earlier. The Federal National Mortgage Association (later to be dubbed Fannie Mae) had been created during the Depression to increase the availability of home loans for middle-income Americans. One way it did that was to create a "secondary" market for mortgages, based in New York and Washington.

Why, you ask, would investors in some distant city be willing to buy mortgages on houses they had never seen that were owned by people whose names they didn't know? Fannie Mae set broad minimum standards for mortgages based on the assessed value of the house, the size of the down payment, the credit rating of the borrowers—you get the idea. Then they bought thousands of mortgages that met their credit-quality standard and sold securities that represented claims on the interest and principle for tiny slices of each mortgage in the big pool. That made it possible for an insurance company in Omaha or a pension fund in Dallas to invest with confidence in, say, $10 million in ten thousand mortgages from California. Some of the mortgages might default, but the risk was predictable—and shared with others who had invested in the same pool.

This secondary market for mortgage-backed securities got a huge boost in 1968 when Fannie Mae was privatized—that is, sold to private investors—and it adopted policies designed to increase its profitability. The pace of expansion further accelerated when Congress created a second private "government-sponsored organization," the Federal Home Loan Mortgage Corporation (Freddie Mac), with the goal of giving Fannie Mae some competition.

Banks discovered they could make more money in originating mortgages than by owning them. They began to sell most of their newly minted mortgages to Fannie, Freddie, and other investment firms for a profit, then use the capital they got back to do it all over again.

If "securitization" transformed high-quality mortgages

into a standardized investment that could be sold and resold like stocks and bonds, why stop there? Why not create packages of riskier mortgages from loans with lower down payments and less creditworthy owners, then sell the resulting "mortgage-backed securities" to investors willing to bear more risk in exchange for more interest? And why should banks, which had largely switched from investing in mortgages to creating them, get all the action? Why not let specialized mortgage brokers find the home buyers, create the mortgages, and sell them to Fannie or Freddie or a private investment firm that would repackage them as mortgage-backed securities?

Why not, indeed. And for a long time, it looked like a good deal all around. Home buyers, especially those with modest incomes and less than perfect credit, now had a choice of lenders and lending terms. Institutional investors—pension funds, bank trust departments, insurance companies, mutual funds, even foreign governments—got to quench their voracious appetites for what seemed to be relatively safe investments that paid more interest than, say, a bond issued by Shell Oil or the U.S. Treasury. In 2001, new issues of mortgage-backed securities reached an astounding $1 trillion.

Wait, it gets better. Mortgage-backed securities created other new opportunities to make big bucks. Uncle Sam had been insuring the timely payment of home mortgages for middle-income families since the Great Depression of the 1930s, charging lenders a small premium for the guarantee. Fannie Mae and Freddie Mac continued the practice of insuring the mortgages behind the mortgage-backed securities they created and sold.

The credit insurance side of the business proved lucrative. With house prices rising by 50 percent between 2000 and 2005, homeowners who couldn't afford their monthly payments usually had the option of refinancing their mortgages instead of defaulting. The prospect of easy profits in guaranteeing mortgage repayments lured other investment firms into the act. Giant insurance companies such as AIG dived into the mortgage insurance business. While they were at it, these firms couldn't resist extending similar "credit enhancement" services in any direction the market pointed.

You want to guarantee the repayment of your $5 million loan to Company X five years from now? Just write a check to the Acme Insurance and Storm Door Company today for $100,000. The game was so lucrative that it was extended far beyond the sales of credit enhancements to the actual creditors. You haven't loaned any money to Company Y, but would still like to place a bet that it will default on its bond obligations in ten years? Write us a check now, and we'll pay you $1 million if Company Y does indeed go belly-up.

Once liberated from the necessity of selling services to real creditors and debtors, the credit enhancement business took off like a jackrabbit at a greyhound convention. At its peak in 2007, some $62 *trillion* worth of guarantees were outstanding—a figure that is much larger than all the debt of all the debtors in the world.

Meanwhile, the big investment firms were hiring mathematicians (the insider's term: *quants*) to tailor esoteric new securities from the mortgage-backed securities as well as from other sorts of assets—for example, securitized credit-card debt and securitized car loans. The advantage of these *collateralized debt obligations*, or CDOs, was that they could be sliced and diced in a zillion ways according to when the investors wanted their money back and how much risk they were willing to bear. A CDO might, for example, give the owner a claim on the first 80 percent of the interest on a specific pool of mortgages—a pretty safe bet in most cases. That would leave the claim on the last 20 percent to an investor willing to take much bigger chances.

Of course, the more complicated these securities got, the harder they were for the mere mortals who bought them on behalf of pensioners, life insurance policyholders, etc., to understand. A problem, you say? Yet another opportunity, Wall Street replied.

A handful of companies had long been in the business of assigning credit ratings to newly issued bonds. They made their money by charging the bond issuers for the service. The debt of, say, General Electric might be rated AAA, the highest rating. A successful midsize auto parts manufacturer might only earn a BBB rating ("satisfactory credit at the moment") because it faced growing competition from China and its financial health was linked so closely to the auto-sales roller coaster.

It didn't take a lot of imagination to extend the ratings concept to all manner of newfangled securities—including, of course, the ones backed by home mortgages. This effectively transformed metaphoric black boxes stuffed with only the quants knew what into assets any institutional fund manager thought he/she could understand. So now the Central Bank of China or the pension plan for municipal employees in six small towns in Norway (both real examples) could invest in impossibly complex securities backed some way, somehow, by loans made to, say, homeowners in Riverside, California.

GOOD TIMES MUST END . . .

As the economist Herb Stein once said, "If something cannot go on forever, it will stop." The long boom in housing prices came to a shuddering halt in 2006 and began a steep decline that is apparently not over. Not surprisingly, housing developers and real estate brokers have been badly hurt, as have their employees and the myriad industries supplying everything from lumber to appliances to the bloated housing sector.

But this had all happened before—in fact, it seems to happen every fifteen to twenty years. And while in the past the deflation of housing bubbles had led to real hardship for lots of people, housing busts didn't bring the mighty American financial industry to its knees. What was different this time around?

The bubble did inflate faster this time and affected housing prices in more regional markets. But the mega-shock was largely a consequence of changes in Wall Street that left all the big players (not to mention the rest of us) far more vulnerable to surprises.

NASTY SURPRISES

Bankers Don't Act like Bankers Anymore

When banks retained the mortgages they originated, they had a strong interest in making sure that borrowers kept up their payments—or at least invested large enough down payments to protect the creditors in the event of foreclosure. During this last housing boom, however, most mortgages were quickly sold to investment firms to be repackaged as securities. As long as somebody would buy them, bankers weren't too picky about to whom they extended the credit.

That explains why banks were happy to make even "liar's loans"—mortgages in which the applicants were required to declare their income, but the banks promised not to check whether they were fibbing. Still, why didn't the investment firms that bought the mortgages pay more attention to the risk they would never be repaid? Because these firms didn't have much incentive to care either, as long as somebody would buy the mortgage-backed securities from them.

This goes on and on. Why were the pension funds, mutual funds, insurance companies, etc., willing to buy all those mortgage-backed securities without really knowing what stood behind them? Because Freddie Mac or Fannie Mae or some big insurance company such as AIG was willing to guarantee repayment, or one of the credit agencies was willing to bless the securities with a high rating.

Wait; this has to end somewhere. Why was it so easy to obtain high credit ratings and credit insurance? That is a real puzzle. The best answer is that the people in these organizations who were in charge of judging the credit quality worried more about this year's performance bonuses than about keeping their jobs when the brown stuff hit the fan. Or maybe their bosses had made it clear that they wouldn't keep their jobs long enough to care unless they generated huge fees by giving good ratings or writing insurance for mortgage-backed securities.

Garbage In, Garbage Out

Sophisticated mathematical models for "pricing" risk, rendered practical by the blinding speed of modern computers, made tons of money for forward-thinking investment firms in the 1980s and 1990s in markets for new sorts of securities. So, few money managers had qualms about trusting the wisdom of the quants who designed all those unfathomably complex mortgage-backed securities and kept their firms' exposure to financial risk at bay.

But the computer models were no better than the weakest assumptions on which they were based. All too often they assumed that, in a pinch, (a) there would always be someone to buy the securities at their fair market value, and (b) everyone with an excellent credit record who owed money to their firms would be able to pay it back. With hindsight, both assumptions seem foolish. But how do you argue with a guy who made a billion dollars for the company last year simply by writing some fancy computer software?

The Bosses No Longer Understand Their Own Businesses

Investment bankers have never been shy about explaining how much brainpower goes into their operations. But until quite recently, success in the business really turned in large part on salesmanship, old-boy connections, and a willingness to work eighty-hour weeks. So the people who got to the top were rarely the ones who majored in math as undergraduates or spent their time at business school studying nonlinear optimization modeling.

As investment firms grew increasingly dependent on complicated financial models, the people in charge lost the ability to ask the right questions or even to pick the right people to ask the right questions. So they were caught off guard when things turned sour in 2007. They lost precious months catching up with reality as their businesses stumbled toward the brink.

What goes for investment company executives, by the way, applies to the regulators, too. Most of the enforcement staff were far better equipped to deal with familiar problems—accounting fraud and failure to meet legal disclosure requirements—than to recognize the risks in holding or insuring collateralized debt obligations. And their bosses, typically political appointees, didn't have a clue.

There's (Still) No Free Lunch in Financial Leverage

Archimedes, ancient Greece's Renaissance man fifteen hundred years before the Renaissance, is credited with saying, "Give me a place to stand, and with a lever I will move the whole world." The same principle applies to finance.

Try this example. If you loan out a dollar from your pocket at 10 percent interest, you end up with $1.10 a year later. But suppose instead you choose to "lever" the dollar by borrowing an extra $100 at 9 percent interest and lending out the entire $101 to others at 10 percent interest. Now, after you pay back the money you owe at 9 percent interest, you'll end up with $2.10—a whopping 110 percent return on the dollar of your own that you invested.

Leverage is thus the real deal for anyone in the business of making serious money as a lender. Regulated commercial banks—the kind with government-insured checking accounts—are legally limited in how much they can borrow to make loans. For good reason. Think back to our example. Suppose you lent out the $101, but got back just $90. Instead of making 110 percent on your own dollar, you wouldn't even be able to pay back all you owe. In plain terms, you'd be insolvent.

But the regulations on leverage for other sorts of investment firms are less clear-cut. Back in 2004, when Wall Street still viewed the world as its very own candy box, the five biggest investment firms asked the Securities and Exchange Commission for permission to increase their borrowing without expanding their capital cushions. They got it—and promptly increased their financial leverage to unprecedented levels. For example, by the end of 2007 Bear Stearns was using just $11 billion of its own capital to back close to $400 billion in loans to other firms. So, when the housing bubble burst and even a tiny fraction of that $400 billion seemed at risk of not paying off, The Bear was in big trouble.

Of those five investment firms, Lehman Brothers went bankrupt, Bear Stearns was swallowed by the JP Morgan Chase bank, and Merrill Lynch sold itself to the Bank of America for a pittance. The two strongest, Goldman Sachs and Morgan Stanley, took shelter from the raging storm by transforming themselves into banks that could borrow at will from the Federal Reserve.

It's a Small, Small World After All

Perhaps the nastiest surprise has been how easily and rapidly trouble spread from home mortgages to virtually every other market for credit. That didn't happen in the 1980s, even when hundreds of savings and loan associations went broke and the government was stuck with a $200 billion bill. What explains the difference?

Start with the fact that much of the action in finance has moved from tightly regulated banks to a global network of unregulated markets dominated by the giant investment firms. When the S&L credit crunch came in the 1980s, hardly anybody panicked because most of the money at risk consisted of federally insured deposits that were as safe as U.S. currency. This time around, however, the wealth at risk (investments in mortgage-backed securities) came from a million pockets in virtually every country in the world.

A lot of those investments were, of course, insured—but not by Uncle Sam, the only insurer with unlimited funds to meet its obligations. And nobody really knew which firms were on the hook, or for how much. Indeed, senior executives at Merrill Lynch only belatedly discovered that the firm had insured tens of billions of dollars' worth of mortgage-backed securities in an effort to find buyers for them once the market had begun to turn sour.

What's more, it soon became apparent that credit-insurance liabilities were spread far beyond the usual suspects. As noted earlier, insurance companies had joined Freddie Mac, Fannie Mae, and a host of other investment firms in guaranteeing trillions of dollars' worth of securities in order to gain billions in up-front premiums. So when housing prices slipped and millions of homeowners were unable to keep up their mortgage payments or to refinance, the dominoes fell in a maddeningly unpredictable order.

Investment firms—even firms that had been reasonably prudent—couldn't borrow against the value of the mortgage-backed securities they owned because nobody knew what the securities were really worth. By the same token, nobody would lend to the insurance companies because nobody knew how much credit insurance they had sold, or how much they would have to pay off.

There's more. Regulated commercial banks weren't immune to the problem because many had found loopholes in the regulations that had allowed them to load up on mortgage-backed securities back when it looked like a way to coin money. Indeed, the credit market had become so tangled that participants were no longer able to distinguish the wheat from the chaff.

Thus began the vicious cycle. Houses became yet harder to sell because bankers were reluctant to give mortgages to even the most creditworthy buyers. Small businesses, which relied on bank lines of credit, were also affected because lenders worried that a recession was looming. As the panic spread, even the value of the short-term securities issued by giant blue-chip corporations that had no exposure to mortgage-backed securities began to be questioned.

Money market funds, which supplied the bulk of the $3 trillion in revolving credit used to finance day-to-day business operations in every industry across the globe, found they couldn't easily sell high-quality, short-term securities they owned when they needed extra cash to pay off their increasingly nervous depositors. Indeed, this critical short-term credit market would probably have collapsed if the government had not agreed to temporarily insure money market fund deposits and to act as a buyer of last resort when the funds couldn't unload securities at full value.

Who's responsible for this mess? The better question is, who isn't?

16

The senior executives of the major investment firms certainly deserve a place high on the dishonor roll. Can you imagine any other industry in which bosses with multimillion-dollar salary packages didn't understand how the products they sell actually work, or how defects in those products could bring down their companies?

Save some blame for federal and state regulators. Sure, they were outgunned in the expertise needed to assess risk on the new Wall Street. Sure, they were right to worry that the heavy hand of regulation could undermine the sort of innovation that has made New York the financial capital of the world. But they were naive to fall back on reassurances that the financial markets would, in the end, correct their own mistakes—that a wildly profitable industry run by the best and the brightest would never risk hurting the goose that laid the golden eggs.

And don't forget the politicians. It's hardly a secret that, in today's Washington (and Albany and Sacramento and Austin) money talks. And nobody talks—make that *shouts*—louder than Wall Street. Probably the biggest mistake Congress made was to allow Freddie Mac and Fannie Mae, which had been created to make it possible for middle-income families to buy houses on reasonable terms, to behave like every other giant investment firm on the hunt for a fast buck.

WHAT DOES IT ALL MEAN FOR *YOU*?

The financial meltdown, alas, is still a work in progress. While Wall Street will obviously never be the same, just how far the government will have to go to bring stability to the financial system is still up in the air. Accordingly, the risks that small-

and medium-size investors face, and the ways in which they can protect themselves (or even profit) from the chaos, are likely to change. Still, a few lessons couldn't be clearer.

Your Broker/Banker/Investment Adviser Is Not Your Friend

It's second nature to distrust roofing contractors and used-car salesmen. But most Americans are all too willing to take professional investment advice at face value.

This crisis has proved how wrongheaded such trust can be. While many, perhaps most, of the people who are paid to help you decide how to invest and how to borrow are conscientious, they are at heart salesmen who generally radiate an optimism that is both infectious and misplaced.

More to the point, their pocketbook interests rarely coincide perfectly with yours. The mortgage broker only gets paid if he gets you to sign on the dotted line, and he won't be there to commiserate when you can't make the monthly payments. The investment adviser may be willing to help you build a sound savings plan, but he'll make a decent living only if he steers you into investments that pay him hefty commissions. The insurance salesman is right to warn you of the dangers of leaving your family without a breadwinner, but the insurance policies he's apt to push are the ones that reward him most generously.

None of this implies that you must plot an investment strategy entirely on your own—hey, you bought this book. But it does put the burden on you to be clearheaded about the limits of advice from experts, and to seek help from sources whose interests more or less mesh with yours.

The Policeman Probably Is Your Friend

I don't mean some guy in blue carrying a Smith & Wesson. In this case, the police are a half-dozen federal agencies ranging from the SEC to the Federal Reserve that are charged with keeping Wall Street stable and honest. For the past two decades, the mantra of mainstream economists has been "disclosure trumps regulation"—that is, it's far better to demand that bankers and brokers lay out exactly what they're selling than to play nanny by limiting the risks investors and borrowers are permitted to take.

As one of those economists, I'm not unsympathetic. Too often in the past, regulators have ended up defending entrenched interests at the expense of the public. But it's an understatement to say that, this time around, the approach didn't work out.

For one thing, Wall Street never delivered on its promise to disclose risk. The big investment firms almost made a game of avoiding disclosure, hiding risk in myriad ways. Indeed, they were so good at it that they concealed the risk even from key decision-makers within the firms. (Otherwise, Lehman Brothers would still be in business.) For another, we've found out the hard way that the mistakes made by hotshot investment managers reaching for bigger bonuses can cost others their jobs and their savings.

Probably most important, we've learned that there's a limit to what you can ask of ordinary Americans, who find that investing their savings or shopping for a mortgage is as daunting as taking the SATs. After all, somewhere in the documents signed by every home buyer who accepted mortgage terms he or she couldn't possibly afford was all the bad news he or she didn't want to hear.

All that's about to change. The big question now is whether the regulators will have the resources to do an adequate job of policing, as well as the discretion and wisdom to let free markets do their thing when they are working well.

Herd Instincts Are Powerful

Every time a bubble bursts, hindsight makes it clear just how stupidly investors behaved—especially near the end. Think, for example, of how absurd it was to speculate in Miami condos in 2005, when prices had already reached the point that most people couldn't afford to live in them and the city skyline was cluttered with a dozen apartment buildings under construction. Or how nutty it was to take out a mortgage on a house in San Diego if the only way you could make the payments was to refinance the mortgage when the house became more valuable.

On second thought, *stupid* is the wrong word. Going along with the crowd is a potent—and in many cases useful—instinct. Do you really want to wait until you see the saber-toothed tiger with your own eyes before you make a run for it? So the trick is to think independently about investments, to resist the impulse to do what everyone else is doing because people made so much money doing it last year.

Fear Is an Expensive Emotion

What should you do when the stock market takes a nosedive and those mutual fund shares you bought for $20 are worth only $15? How should I know? Every day is a new day on Wall

Street. Just because the market went down today doesn't make it more likely it will go down tomorrow. By the same token, today's tumble doesn't make an uptick more likely.

What I do know, though, is that fear breeds overreaction. Investors who are amateurs—investors such as you who are accumulating savings for college expenses, retirement, maybe a vacation home—are rarely as well informed as the professionals who move the market. Indeed, it used to be a popular (if not terribly successful) strategy on Wall Street to watch what small investors did, then do the opposite. The bottom line: invest for the long run, resisting the inclination to jump ship the minute the storm hits.

TWO

After the Fall

RETHINKING INVESTMENT BASICS

In one sense, nothing has changed. The goal of investing is still to get the most from your savings, bearing in mind that all but the most conservative strategies involve risk. To increase the chances of making more money, you have to take the chance that you'll make less.

But that and a dime will get you a thimbleful of Starbucks. While the goal remains the same, the means to this end need to be rethought in light of the shocking meltdown on Wall Street and the rapid spread of the credit crisis to every corner of the economy. Here I'll outline some basics. Later chapters will flesh out the story with specific advice on where to put your money now, and why.

THE PRICE OF LUNCH

Everyone's heard the aphorism "there's no such thing as a free lunch," but relatively few, I would guess, know where it came from. The "free lunch" was a tradition in late nineteenth-century America, perhaps originating in San Francisco in the lean years following the California gold rush. To attract customers, taverns would offer a modest selection of luncheon goodies to anyone willing to buy a nickel beer. The lunch was free only in the sense that it was included in the cost of the suds. The taverns depended on most customers not stopping at one mug.

Milton Friedman, the great economist, coined the maxim in explaining why, when an economy is operating at full tilt, the only way to give more to some people is to give less to others. But lately, it's being used to illuminate the trade-off between risk and return in investing—and to chastise investors who naively bought into the idea that the buffet (read "mortgage-backed securities") didn't come with a bar bill attached. The real questions for investors, postmeltdown, are how much lunch actually costs now, and whether they can afford to buy it. To put it more directly, how much can you expect to increase the return on your investment by taking bigger chances of losing, and are you prepared to accept the risk?

One way of looking at the proliferation of newfangled investment products in the last few years is that too many investors "underpriced" risk—that is, they either didn't understand how much risk they shouldered in holding investment products, or they miscalculated the consequences of losing. The most likely effect, postmeltdown: investors will go too far in the other direction, overpricing risk at least until the memories of 2008 fade.

That's terrible news for the economy: rapid economic growth depends on the willingness of investors to gamble on innovation. But it is good news for the intrepid: if most investors are now far less willing to bear risk, anyone who is prepared to take chances should be able to invest in risky assets on attractive terms. This explains why Warren Buffett, the world's richest man, has placed $5 billion bets on General Electric and Goldman Sachs. If Goldman Sachs and GE (which, by the way, is deeply involved in the lending business through its GE Capital subsidiary) prosper, Buffett and the stockholders of his company (Berkshire Hathaway) will laugh all the way to the bank. It also explains why you've probably been hearing about new investment funds that are specializing in buying distressed assets at fire-sale prices.

The likelihood that Buffett and company are right—that the financial markets are now inclined to overprice risk—poses a dilemma for small investors. On the one hand, the meltdown has made it all too clear how far and how quickly markets can decline, and how few of us can afford to bet the store (and the house and the kids' education) that it won't happen again. On the other, the collapse has plainly created opportunities for buying securities at far less than they will sell for in a few years. In later chapters I'll discuss the nuts and bolts of finding the middle ground, of investing in ways that make it possible to share in the likely market comeback without taking imprudent chances with your savings.

THE ILLUSION OF CREDIT INSURANCE

Ask the managers of pension funds, mutual funds, bank trust departments, and the like why they bet heavily on risky mortgage-backed securities, and they'll explain that the investments weren't really so risky. Most, after all, were insured by Freddie Mac, Fannie Mae, or one of several dozen other reputable investment firms and insurance companies. The $62 trillion question, then, is why the insurance has proved so worthless.

One reason is that the sort of insurance the managers bought wasn't regulated. Companies that sell, say, fire insurance must meet state regulators' standards, the most important of which is keeping an adequate capital cushion to cover liabilities in the event of a worst-case claim. In the vast majority of cases, the "insurance" covering fixed-return securities such as bonds and mortgage-backed securities technically wasn't insurance at all, so the government had no say in how much capital the insurers set aside for claims.

Still, you would expect the companies that sold insurance for securities to protect themselves. They did—but not by accumulating adequate reserves that could be used to meet their obligations. They did it the new-fashioned way, spreading around the risk by purchasing insurance from other investment firms to cover the insurance they'd sold. The catch, of course, is that the buck had to stop somewhere, and by most calculations the insurers weren't collectively prepared to cover the cost of mortgage defaults that could exceed $1 trillion. Actually, there was a second catch: many of the insurance contracts probably were enforceable. But the daisy chain of insurer to insurer to insurer had become so complex and so inaccessible to public scrutiny that, once the housing market turned sour, nobody (except the federal government) was willing to lend money to the investment companies involved.

Don't look now, but another shoe here is left to fall. For decades, a handful of firms have specialized in insuring municipal bonds—the bonds issued by state and local governments, as well as by public-purpose agencies such as nonprofit hospitals. It's been a great business, thus far: since the Depression, few municipal bonds have defaulted. But the insurers maintain only modest reserves, and in a systemwide crisis—think nasty, nasty recession—the insurers might not be able to cover their obligations.

New regulation requiring disclosure of credit-insurance liabilities and probably insisting on adequately funded reserves will surely reduce the chances of another debacle like the last. But the emphasis should be on the word *last*. The new regulations are bound to make it far more expensive to sell credit insurance, creating an incentive for somebody to figure a way around the regulation.

So where does that leave ordinary investors? Some privately insured securities may still be worth buying at the right price, but not because they are insured. The only credit insurance that can absolutely, positively be counted on is insurance issued by the folks who print money. That, of course, means the federal government. But it also means the governments of countries with strong currencies and lots of cash reserves. More about that in later chapters.

THE VALUE OF DIVERSIFICATION

You've heard the spiel umpteen times: don't put all your investment eggs in one basket. This is common sense—baskets sometimes leak.* But it's also solid, sophisticated economics. Diversification creates opportunities to reduce risk without

---

* Break . . . develop holes . . . I guess I've worn out the metaphor.

reducing the expected return (and vice versa). That's why professionals always recommend that small investors buy a broad range of investments—for example, buying mutual funds that own multiple stocks rather than buying a handful of individual stocks on their own.

But diversification is a little trickier than you might think. If the bad news that could affect one investment equally affects another, buying both won't generate the something-for-nothing benefits of true diversification. The current financial crisis we've just experienced suggests that some kinds of bad news can adversely affect virtually every investment possible.

Think about it. First housing prices began to fall, dragging down the value of companies that build houses, finance them, and insure their mortgages. But the holdings of mortgage-related securities were so widespread (and the risks so poorly understood) that the housing bust devastated huge swaths of financial services industries in Europe as well as in the United States. The resulting credit crunch threatened all sorts of businesses on every continent, cratering stock prices in Brazil, India, and Russia as well as the United States.

This doesn't imply that investors should stop bothering to seek diversification. But it should make them seek diversification in less familiar places—for example, in government securities denominated in foreign currencies. More generally, it should make them more cautious in relying on diversification to contain risk. The bottom line: now, more than ever, most investors need a rock-solid core of virtually riskless assets in their portfolios.

THE PROSPECT OF INFLATION

Inflation, the monster that eroded savings, distorted investment, and turned union wage negotiations into a game of chicken in the 1970s, virtually vanished overnight in the early 1980s after Federal Reserve chairman Paul Volcker declared that nothing (including a deep recession) would stand between the Fed and stable prices. There has been little reason to doubt the Fed's priorities ever since.

The current crisis doesn't directly test the credibility of the Fed's commitment to containing inflation. Far from it: the meltdown of the financial system is the opposite of inflationary. While the measures the Fed has taken to ease the credit crunch would be inflationary in ordinary times, there is no danger that low, low interest rates will lead to the shortages of raw materials and labor that are a prerequisite to rising prices.

In fact, some economists have voiced concerns that the American economy will get stuck in a "liquidity trap" in which banks plow all that cash the Fed is pressing on them into ultrasafe U.S. Treasury securities, rather than lending it to capital-starved businesses. This is not a theoretical concern: it happened in Japan in the 1990s after the financial system was decimated by a collapse in real estate prices.

So why do I even bring up the subject here? If I were convinced that deflation, not inflation, was the long-term danger, it would change how I invest. The Japanese economy didn't grow for twelve years, and in most of those years consumer prices actually fell. Japan went from the world's industrial powerhouse to an also-ran playing second fiddle to China in the Asian economy. So the best investments proved to be long-term bonds that guaranteed a decent fixed return far into the future while the cost of living fell.

But America's problems aren't really the same as Japan's. While there is little or no danger of inflation in the next few years, all signs point to inflationary pressures down the road. Start with the fact that Americans spend far more abroad than they sell. The only way this can continue is for foreigners to accept IOUs—the Chinese government alone holds over $1 trillion in U.S. government securities. One day foreigners will balk, leading to a fall in the exchange value of the dollar and a rise in the price of everything from Korean cars to Chinese TVs.

Add to this the U.S. budget deficit. Economists may argue about the impact of the deficits incurred in the Bush years. But nobody denies that, a decade from now, the deficit will explode under the pressure of rising outlays for Medicare. That will force Washington to choose between sharp cuts in benefits, gigantic increases in taxes—and inflation.

From this perspective, the current financial meltdown is a distraction masking the growing prospect that inflation will once again become as American as apple pie. Prudent investors should plan accordingly.

THE CURSE OF LEVERAGE

Financial leverage, at heart, is a way to use other people's money to do the heavy lifting. It explains, in large part, how captains of finance can rapidly get rich. The recipe is simple enough: borrow a billion at 9 percent and invest it at a higher return. If you earn 10 percent on the investment, you get to keep $10 million a year after expenses. The catch, of course—and the simplest explanation for why the mortgage mess decimated Wall Street—is that if you earn just 8 percent (instead of 10) you owe $10 million at the end of the year.

In most times and places, the agonies and ecstasies of leverage largely affect the rich, because lenders are reluctant to extend credit to anyone who lacks the deep pockets to pay them back. But during the housing boom lenders threw caution to the winds, offering mortgages for which borrowers didn't need to put up a penny of their own. Suddenly middle-income Americans by the millions were enjoying the perks of leverage. As long as the return on the asset—the rate of appreciation of the house—was higher than the interest rate on the mortgage, the house effectively cost the owner nothing. All he/she had to do was to occasionally borrow a little more against the rising value of the house and use the cash to make the interest payments.

Of course, this hasn't worked out any better for highly leveraged homeowners than it did for the mega-leveraged stockholders of Bear Stearns and Lehman Brothers. For better or worse (mostly better) it's a safe bet that no-money-down, borrow-your-monthly-payment mortgages won't be offered again anytime soon.

But leverage, with its potential to turbocharge your investment returns or to slam them into the gutter, still lurks in a variety of places. Many businesses still live and breathe on leverage—for example, the commercial real estate industry, where the property that generates their income is typically encumbered with huge mortgages. Likewise, many retailers use credit to finance the cars on their lot, the jewelry in their display cases, the suits on the racks. Thus the returns in such industries will be more volatile in times when both the cost of borrowing and the availability of loans is problematic.

This doesn't mean that you should avoid every leveraged investment in every circumstance. And it sure doesn't mean you should save up the full cost of a house before buying one.

But in an era in which all investing has apparently grown riskier, it pays more than ever to be cautious about borrowing.

THE LOGIC OF HOMEOWNERSHIP

Speaking of houses, the mortgage-market mess has made people reluctant to buy for three reasons.

First, just as Americans worried about *not* buying a house while the market was rising lest they become priced out of reach, now they fear buying a house that could be worth 10–20 percent less next year or the next. Second, they know that it is harder to qualify for a mortgage than it was a few years ago. Virtually all lenders expect you to pony up a substantial down payment. None that I know about are prepared to make home loans with low initial teaser rates, or to make loans in which the borrower need not document his income, or to permit "negative amortization" loans in which the principal you owe actually increases over the first few years. Third, people now rightly perceive that housing prices are volatile—that an investment in a house is far riskier than, say, an investment in a bank CD. In uncertain times, why take the chance?

All that's true as far as it goes. But there's a critical difference between a house that you live in and other investments (including houses you don't live in): most of the "returns" consist of the value of living there. So owning the house you live in produces a predictable return. Choosing to rent rather than to own, however, doesn't actually reduce the volatility of your wealth. You've got to live somewhere, so an increase/decrease in rents effectively reduces/raises the buying power of your assets—a change in wealth by another name.

It's also worth remembering that the tax laws still favor homeowners over renters. Renters pay taxes on their income, so rent comes from after-tax dollars. Homeowners, by contrast, can deduct their mortgage payments from their taxable incomes, so their primary out-of-pocket expense for housing comes from pretax dollars. What's more, if you sell the house you've been living in for a profit, there's no tax on up to $500,000 in gains (per couple). By contrast, a renter who profits from any investment (including houses that other people live in) is liable for taxes on the gain.

Let's be clear here. It doesn't make sense for everyone with an adequate income and the savings for a down payment to buy their house. Houses are far less liquid than many other investments—that is, even in good times it can be difficult to find a buyer quickly at the fair market value. Consider, too, that the expense of buying and selling a house (the brokerage commissions, the up-front financing fees) are far larger than transaction costs for securities that are traded on exchanges. So if you, say, planned to move to Tahiti in a year or two, a house would be a problematic investment.

But the experience of this latest housing boom and bust hasn't changed the fundamentals. For people who can afford it, owner-occupied housing remains a prime place to put your money.

TOO MUCH ATTENTION TO INVESTMENTS IS AS PROBLEMATIC AS TOO LITTLE

Most investment firms don't hold securities for long. Indeed, one of the most reliable ways they have to make money is to buy and sell securities quickly, earning pennies per share, but making it up in volume. While such activities are sometimes dismissed as "speculation," their willingness to buy and sell on small changes in price is what makes it possible for you to sell securities almost instantly without getting hosed.

But what's good for financial markets as a whole isn't necessarily good for individual investors—especially small investors. Trading securities isn't like, say, roulette, where the odds of winning are always against you. It's more like poker at a casino, where the house takes a little bit of every pot for its troubles. So, on average, securities buyers and sellers as a group lose a little bit on every transaction.

Actually, it's not always so small a chunk. While the commissions you pay on sales and purchases of securities listed on exchanges are generally modest (and plain to see), investors in less frequently traded securities, such as municipal bonds and bank CDs offered through securities brokers, are pretty much at the mercy of the "market maker"—typically investment firms that specialize in particular sorts of securities. What's more, you never know how much you've paid for the transaction because you never know how much the party at the other end of the deal is paying or collecting.

Turning over assets quickly in the hope of buying low and selling high has never made sense for investors without millions to bet. Indeed, when investment managers paid to oversee other people's money "churn" portfolios to generate commission income for themselves, they are violating the securities laws. What, then, has changed since the market meltdown?

The temptations to trade excessively are higher because the financial markets are more volatile. Just imagine if you'd bought Goldman Sachs stock the day before Warren Buffett recapitalized the company, then sold it the day after! (But, of course, for every winner in such transactions, there's a loser.) Worse, the costs of trading are higher because, in many cases, the markets for the assets have become less liquid. So if frequent trading was a mistake before the meltdown, it's a bigger mistake now.

I wish I could draw a bright line between buying and selling securities in a prudent effort to maximize returns or to minimize losses on the one hand, and trading for trading's sake on the other. What is pretty clear is that investing with a time horizon of days or months is asking for trouble.

ACCOUNTING FOR TAXATION

Federal tax law is designed to encourage investors to hold their assets for more than a year by taxing gains (if there are any) at a lower rate. In 2009 and 2010, such "long-term" capital gains will be taxed at 15 percent for middle- and upper-income families (instead of 28 percent or more on wages). Families with modest incomes (below $65,000) pay no tax at all on gains (as compared to 10–15 percent on ordinary income).

The capital gains rates are slated to go up after 2010, but will still provide a break for people willing to hold assets for a while. Besides, there's good reason to believe that the current tax breaks will be extended past 2010—perhaps for everyone, and likely for families with incomes below $250,000.

So, on first look, it paid to invest for the long haul before the crash, and nothing's changed in the crash's wake. But, on second look, that's not so clear. There's always been a risk that holding assets you didn't want to own in order to qualify for lower capital gains taxes would be a mistake—that the tax savings would be more than offset by the decline in the asset's value when you did get around to selling. And now that risk is greater if you believe, as I do, that securities markets will remain more volatile in the wake of the meltdown.

Taxes still matter in decisions about selling assets. But they should matter a little less now than they did before the bottom fell out.

BUILDING A RETIREMENT NEST EGG

In the best of possible worlds, people save enough between the time their children are grown and retirement to maintain their living standards after ceasing to work. Just how much is enough is a matter of controversy, though, even among experts. But there's good reason to believe that roughly two baby boomers out of three are not on a trajectory to retire well.

The mortgage meltdown changed things in three ways, none of them for the better. First, an awful lot of people were counting on the value of their house to see them through—that is, planning to downsize when they retired and use the proceeds on golf, cruises, and hip replacements. They probably still own those houses, but they are worth a lot less than they were premeltdown. And if the houses are mortgaged, as most are, the effect of leverage (see above) has disproportionately reduced owners' wealth.

Second, the financial crisis has led the Federal Reserve to cut interest rates, reducing returns on conservative investments such as government-insured bank CDs. And if rates stay low for years, which wouldn't be surprising, the pace at which earnest savers can accumulate wealth for retirement will slow.

Third, the collapse of Wall Street has probably increased the volatility of securities markets. Yet, as the baby boomers get older, their willingness to bear risk to increase their investment returns will (and should) fall. So they won't be in a position to take advantage of high-risk, potentially high-return investments that could build savings faster.

There's no way to sugarcoat this. As a result of the financial meltdown—the onetime loss in the value of houses and other investments, and the economic climate that has followed it—people will have to work longer and spend less of their incomes if they hope to live well in retirement. The one bright spot here is that the meltdown may serve as a wake-up call for younger Americans, who have more time to adjust their spending habits.

YOU'RE STILL YOUR OWN BEST ASSET

Corny? Sure, but truer than ever. In thinking about investments, most people think no further than a house and a brokerage account full of securities. But education and skills training—what economists call human capital—represent the best possible investment for many. I don't mean that in the "isn't education great for the soul" sense. The average returns to a college education in terms of lifetime earning power have been higher than the return on stocks for at least three decades. So in an era in which the returns on conventional investments are likely to be more volatile than ever, education remains a winner.

That said, there's increasing evidence that the returns to education are unevenly distributed—not everyone who finishes college shares in the bounty. This suggests two things.

First, it pays to be aware of the sorts of jobs this degree or that is really likely to qualify you for. Second, the returns to graduate education in a technical field are probably more predictable than the returns to a college degree—and, on average, probably higher.

THREE

Bulletproofing Your Savings

Okay, time for the nitty-gritty—what you need to do to protect your savings from the sorts of surprises that brought down some (well, most) of the great investments firms along with the best and brightest in the business.

A few years ago, I would hardly have bothered to provide this information in such detail. All of these investments seemed safe, and the real distinctions between them came from other considerations: convenience, liquidity needs, taxes. My guess is that all of these investments are still safe enough—that Washington would now do whatever it takes to prevent the black hole that was Wall Street from sucking the value out of these conservative investments. But, in the spirit of "once burned, shame on you; twice burned, shame on me," I'm laying out even the small risks in detail.

BANK CHECKING, NOW, AND SAVINGS ACCOUNTS

Money in checking accounts that don't pay interest in commercial banks, or savings and loans, is now insured. Period, full stop. If your bank can't meet its obligations, the Federal Deposit Insurance Corporation, a government agency that as a practical matter has bottomless pockets, will pay you back. Typically when banks fail, depositors don't even find out about it until the FDIC has merged the dying institution with a healthy bank and transferred the insured accounts to the new fold.

The blanket guarantee for non-interest-bearing deposits ends on December 31, 2009. If the dust has settled by then, Washington may decide to return the insured limit to $250,000 or even $100,000. So pay attention if you plan to keep more than $100,000 in a single bank. Careless depositors have lost roughly $250 million in failed banks in the past few decades because their accounts exceeded the insured maximum.

I said that checking deposits can't earn interest. That's true, but easily gotten round—provided you're willing to settle for some limit on how much money is insured against bank failure.

Back in the 1970s, when small banks were losing the battle for depositor dollars to large banks, their lawyers invented the "negotiated order of withdrawal" (NOW) account.* This is just a federally insured checking account by another name that is permitted to pay interest. In the 1980s, virtually all

---

* Banks hardly ever use the lingo, but every interest-paying bank checking account is really a NOW account.

banks got on board in order to compete with newly popular interest-paying money market funds. More recently, a handful of banks have blazed another trail to the same end, creating insured savings accounts that are linked to regular checking accounts, making it more convenient to keep cash in higher-yield savings until you really need it.

If NOW accounts can do everything a checking account can do and still pay interest, why would anyone with less than $250,000 to deposit opt for plain old checking? NOW accounts often require higher minimum balances to avoid monthly account maintenance fees. What's more, banks usually throw in some goodies for regular checking-account customers (free check printing, perhaps a small interest-rate break on loans) that NOW customers don't get. Note, too, that any interest you earn on a NOW account is taxable income, while fees charged to accounts are not deductible from taxable income unless the account is used only for business.

Typically, the interest earned on NOW accounts is less than the fees you can avoid with regular checking unless you maintain an average balance of several thousand dollars. But there are some exceptions—notably, with online banks that aggressively troll cyberspace for deposits.

There's absolutely nothing fishy, by the way, about online banks—they're federally regulated and insured. Most include access to some earthbound bank's ATM machines at no cost. But there are drawbacks. Many won't allow you to write checks—cash withdrawals must be made through ATMs, and all payments must be electronic transfers. If you do need to pay someone by check, you have to maintain a checking account somewhere else. Note, too, that online banks lack branches to visit for, say, a bank officer's signature on a legal document. Also, bricks-and-mortar banks sometimes offer a friendly face to cut you a break when you bounce a check.

If you have the slightest reason to doubt that your bank account is, indeed, federally insured, the FDIC maintains a search service online to check. Just go to www2.fdic.gov/idasp/main_bankfind.asp.

*Banks Paying High Interest Rates on NOW
and Linked Savings Accounts*

Bear in mind that this list isn't exhaustive, and that bank policies change frequently.

SalemFiveDirect
An online subsidiary of a Massachusetts bank that fairly consistently pays high rates on no-strings, federally insured NOW accounts (eOne accounts). No minimum deposit required, and the bank reimburses you up to $15 a month for fees charged by others banks' ATMs. Visit salemfivedirect.com or call 1-800-322-2265.

BankofInternet
Another online bank consistently offering high interest on NOW accounts. Reimbursements (to $8 a month) to use anybody's ATMs. However, an average balance of $5,000 is required to avoid monthly charges (currently $7.50). Visit bankofinternet.com or call 1-877-541-2634.

UnivestDirect
The online subsidiary of a Philadelphia-area bank. The bank's insured NOW accounts pay decent interest, and there's no

minimum balance needed to escape fees. Free ATM use through the national Allpoint network. One minor drawback: checks cost about nine cents each. Visit univestdirect.com or call 1-877-723-5571.

ING Direct
This online bank subsidiary of a Dutch insurance company offers federally insured NOW accounts (Orange Electric accounts) that exact no monthly maintenance charges, but do not allow you to write paper checks. It also offers savings accounts (Orange Savings) that can be linked electronically to any checking account (including an Orange Electric account). Online transfers from Orange Savings to your checking account take as long as two days. Visit ingdirect.com or call 1-800-ING-DIRECT.

HSBC Direct
Another online subsidiary of a giant global financial services company. It offers federally insured savings accounts that can be linked to any checking account. Account holders use HBSC's huge worldwide ATM network for cash withdrawals and deposits. Note one potential advantage: you can link an HSBC Direct savings account to an HSBC Direct payment account to make electronic payments as well as to a regular HSBC checking account, speeding electronic transfers from savings to checking. Visit hsbcdirect.com or call 1-888-404-4050.

CREDIT UNION ACCOUNTS

Credit unions are nonprofit cooperatives, which exist in a parallel universe to the banks. But in most respects credit union accounts are interchangeable with bank accounts. Interest-earning deposits in federally chartered credit unions are insured by a federal agency, the National Credit Union Share Insurance Fund. As with the FDIC, the agency's resources are, as a practical matter, infinite: you can't lose money in a federally insured credit union account. Note, however:

- Like interest-bearing bank accounts, credit union deposits are only insured to $250,000—a figure that will no doubt return to $100,000 if the FDIC max ratchets back to that number.

- A small minority of credit unions are not federally insured; they are typically backed by state insurance funds with less-than-infinite resources. Federally insured credit unions will display the National Credit Union Association logo. If in doubt about coverage, go to the NCUA's Web site, ncua.gov.

MONEY MARKET FUNDS

The first money market funds appeared in the early 1970s. But they really became popular in the early 1980s, when interest rates hit double digits and banks were prohibited from paying anywhere near the going rate on insured deposits. The idea is simple enough. Sell shares in a mutual fund that invests only in safe, liquid short-term securities that pay fixed rates of interest. Credit the interest to shareholders daily (after taking fees, of course, for your expenses) in the form of more shares. Let shareholders take out cash (that is, redeem shares) with no additional fees by writing checks on the fund. Make sure you always have enough cash on hand to be certain that you don't have to sell the underlying investments in a hurry for less than they are worth.

A few important points. Until the current crisis, nobody insured money market funds against losses associated with declines in the value of their investments. But fund prices have, as a matter of history, been very, very stable. First, to call a fund a "money market" fund the sponsor must invest only in safe securities such as U.S. Treasury securities and the debt of blue-chip corporations, and it must not let the average maturity of the securities exceed ninety days.

Second, most money market funds are sponsored by large investment firms or the umbrella holding companies that own the big commercial banks. They have strong incentives to cover any losses suffered by their money market funds: no investment firm that runs a money market fund wants to put its reputation at risk. Besides, the funds are generally very profitable, and their sponsors want to keep them in business.

So, while no one formally guaranteed that money market share owners would never lose money, it is rare, indeed, when share values go below $1—an event dubbed "breaking the buck." Until last year, it had happened only once (in 1994), when the Community Bankers U.S. Government Fund redeemed shares for ninety-six cents.

Then, on September 16, 2008, two funds (ironically including the very first money market fund, the Reserve Fund) broke the buck after losing money on securities issued by

Lehman Brothers. That triggered a three-day run on money market funds in which frightened investors redeemed $169 billion in shares out of $3.4 trillion outstanding. The panic only ended when the Treasury announced that it would temporarily insure the assets of money market funds as of September 19, 2008, in return for small insurance premiums from the fund managers. A month later it also created an agency that would buy short-term securities from the funds in the event of a credit squeeze. The guaranty program runs to September 19, 2009, but the secretary of the treasury has the option of extending it.

What's the bottom line, then? Are money market funds safe? It's important to keep the incident that triggered the panic in perspective: the two funds that broke the buck still paid back ninety-six to ninety-seven cents per share. Thus, if you had kept money in the Reserve Fund for a year prior to its decision to break the buck, you would have made more in interest than you lost in share value.

It's also worth remembering that sponsors of the really big funds would probably go the last mile to avoid breaking the buck, spending the corporation's money to do it. Then there's the "too big to fail" argument: the Treasury would have an enormous incentive to intervene to prevent the collapse of an industry that provides vital short-term loans to thousands of American corporations.

That said, MM funds should no longer be thought of as the ultimately safe, set-it-and-forget-it investment—a perfect substitute for federally insured bank deposits. I consider it unlikely that anyone will ever lose more than a few percentage points of value in one of these funds. But, then, most people never imagined that Wall Street would be wrecked by a downturn in the housing market.

If you do choose to keep money in a money market fund (and I do), it pays to take some precautions.

- Remember that the federal insurance only covers shares owned on September 19, 2008. New accounts or sums exceeding shares owned on the magic date are not insured.

- Find out whether the sponsor has subscribed to the Treasury guarantee plan by calling or checking its Web site. If it has, you're safe at least until September 2009. If it hasn't, consider using another fund.

- If you're the belt-and-suspenders type, opt for a money market fund that only invests in U.S. Treasury securities (see below), which will never default. The flip side of this little extra bit of safety is that you'll get a lower return—a lot lower return as long as the financial crisis lasts.

- Stick with a fund sponsored by a company with a deep capital cushion of its own, and a brand name to lose (see below).

- Avoid money market funds that cater to high-income clients by investing only in tax-exempt securities issued by states and localities, and in particular avoid those that invest in securities from a single state. The municipal bond market is far less liquid than the market for "commercial paper" issued by big, blue-chip corporations, and thus tax-exempt funds would be more vulnerable in a liquidity crunch. More worrying still, many states and localities could have trouble paying their bills if America experiences a long recession.

- Take a close look at the fund's expenses. Some of the big ones charge as little as .25 percent annually, and there's no reason to believe you are getting anything extra by paying more.

Money Market Funds to Consider

Vanguard Prime Money Market Fund
This gigantic fund (around $100 billion) has low expenses and is run by one of the most reputable, consumer-minded investment firms in the business. The fund is participating in the Treasury guaranty program. Minimum investment: $3,000. Visit vanguard.com or call 1-877-662-7447.

Fidelity Cash Reserves
Another giant MM fund run by a deep-pockets company with a fine reputation. The expenses are a bit higher than for Vanguard Prime, but the average after-expense returns have historically been about the same. Minimum investment: $2,500. Visit fidelity.com or call 1-800-343-3548.

JP Morgan U.S. Government Money Market Fund
Most of the assets are guaranteed by the federal government, and in any case JP Morgan Chase, the sponsor, has signed up the fund for the Treasury guaranty. Minimum investment: $1,000. Visit jpmorganfunds.com or call 1-800-480-4111.

BANK CERTIFICATES OF DEPOSIT (CDS)

The federally insured bank CD is the workhorse of American savings, a safe, predictable addition to the nest eggs of tens of millions of Americans. What you see is what you get, as long as the CD is guaranteed by the Federal Deposit Insurance Corporation. But there is enormous variety in CDs, and investors need to be alert to both the opportunities for earning more interest and the potential downsides in choosing a CD with unusual terms.

Some specifics. CDs are "term deposits"—you specify how long you are willing to lock up the money, and the bank specifies the interest rate it will offer. The terms of most CDs run from six months to five years, while the interest rate is usually fixed when the CD is issued. But the FDIC gives banks wide latitude in setting the length of their commitment (some run as short as one month, some last as long as fifteen years), in determining how the interest rate is set (some ratchet up with time or change along with rates on other securities), in exacting a penalty for early withdrawal (the FDIC insists on a minimum of seven days' worth of interest, but some banks collect as much as six months' interest). Hey, the sky's the limit: banks can (and have) linked the returns on federally insured CDs to indexes ranging from oil prices to the dollar's exchange rate with various foreign currencies.

The vast majority of CDs permit you to cash them before they mature (after paying a penalty), but the contract doesn't give the bank the right to terminate the arrangement before the date of maturity. That's good for you, since it leaves you the option of liquidating a CD early and buying a new one if interest rates rise. But, of course, this arrangement is bad for the bank.

By contrast, some bank CDs sold through securities brokers do give the issuer the right to "call" the CD after a year or two. Such CDs are not necessarily bad investments—the issuing banks usually offer higher interest rates in exchange for your acceptance of the call provision. But you need to understand that your money will likely be handed back just when the opportunities for reinvesting the proceeds in another high-interest CD are lowest.

Most CDs come in $1,000 slices. But banks are free to set lower (or much higher) minimums. Some banks are happy to pay extra interest for "jumbo" CDs—that is, CDs over $100,000. But take care here: FDIC insurance is limited to $250,000 per owner per bank, and that limit will ratchet back to $100,000* at the end of 2009 unless Congress extends the new, enriched maximum. It makes a lot of sense, then, to spread the money among many banks if your savings top the insurance max.

Note, too, that the bank issuing the CD has wide discretion in how frequently it makes interest payments, and whether it "compounds" the interest—that is, pays interest on the interest accumulating within the account. This matters for two reasons. First, the CD paying the highest rate may not actually pay the highest return. Happily, the FDIC requires banks to disclose the one number that does make direct comparison possible—the APY, which is short for "annual percentage yield."

Second, the FDIC insurance limits apply to the total funds an individual has in the bank. Interest that has accumulated, but has not been paid out, counts against the limit. Generally this won't matter. But some CDs work like U.S. savings

---

* The one exception: insured deposits in retirement accounts.

bonds (see 54), paying the interest only when the CD matures or is prematurely cashed. Here, the difference between the amount initially invested and the value of the mature CD can be quite large. For example, $225,000 accumulating at 5 percent interest for five years would lead to a payoff at maturity of a bit more than $287,000—$37,000 more than the current insured maximum.

Interest on CDs, incidentally, is subject to income tax in the year the interest is earned—not the year it is actually paid. So, if you have the sort of CD that accumulates interest within the deposit, expect the bank to report the interest earnings to Uncle Sam even if you have yet to see a penny of it.

Buying CDs Directly from Banks

The rates paid by banks vary widely, by as much as two or three percentage points. Some pay little, exploiting the ignorance or laziness of customers who have failed to shop around. Other banks rely on CDs to generate much of the money they use to make loans and pay top rates to generate an ample supply of cash.

Since all CDs are equally protected against default by the FDIC, you should feel reasonably comfortable about buying an insured CD from any bank, anywhere. You can double-check that the bank really is insured by going to the FDIC's Bank Find Web site: www2.fdic.gov/idasp/main_bankfind .asp.

That said, you should understand the modest downsides in lending money to a bank that is close to insolvency. The FDIC insures your money, but need not honor the terms of the CD. So if a bank goes belly-up, the agency can terminate the CD before maturity and mail you a check for the principal and any interest owed to date. Thus you could have to look for a new place to put your money, and at a lower interest rate.

One way of shopping for CDs is to read the newspaper ads. A far better way is to go to one of a handful of Web sites that keep day-to-day track of the highest-yielding CDs at a variety of maturities. (The Web sites make money by charging fees for click-through referrals to individual banks, as well as by selling on-site advertising.) My favorite site, bankrate.com, also lists the best deals on other bank savings options, as well as on mortgages and credit cards.

Buying CDs through Securities Brokers

Back in the early 1980s, when savings and loan associations were given the green light by Congress to compete with commercial banks in providing loans to just about anybody, many aimed at building deposits far faster than would be possible if they relied solely on local depositors. They worked out deals in which a big brokerage house would buy, say, a $100 million CD from an S&L. Then the broker would cut it up into bite-size pieces and resell the pieces to clients around the world. The slices were insured by the FDIC as long as each was smaller than the maximum insurable amount. The savings and loan boom ended badly (it cost Uncle Sam $200 billion to bail out the S&L's), but the arrangement in which brokers could package insured bank CDs for their retail customers is still with us. And it may be to your advantage to buy CDs in this way.

For starters, brokers offer an easy way to invest up to $50 million (!!!) in fully insured CDs—no need to go from bank to bank to buy insured CDs if you want to invest more than the maximum insurable amount. Second, brokered CDs can be sold through brokers like stocks and bonds—no need to pay a penalty for early redemption. Third, the rates offered on brokered CDs are often a bit higher than the rates you get by buying directly from banks. To go this route, you do need to set up an account with a broker. But that's no more trouble than buying a CD directly from a bank.

So what's the catch? Brokered CDs cannot be redeemed before maturity. So to cash out prematurely, you need to sell the CD through the broker at a price determined by the market. If interest rates have gone up substantially since you bought the CD, the price you'll get in the market could be well below what you paid. Also since brokered CDs come in a wide variety of flavors, you've got to pay attention to the terms. For example, some brokered CDs have the aforementioned "call" features, permitting the issuing bank to give you back your money before the maturity date.

Most securities brokers sell CDs, but it probably makes sense to buy them from a large, well-established broker most likely to have a wide selection on offer and least likely to try to sell you a CD that doesn't qualify for FDIC coverage. Here are a few that fit the bill:

Vanguard. Visit vanguard.com or call 1-877-662-7447.

Raymond James Financial. Visit raymondjames.com or call 1-800-248-8863.

Charles Schwab. Visit schwab.com or call 1-866-232-9890.

Fidelity. Visit fidelity.com or call 1-800-343-3548.

EE U.S. SAVINGS BONDS

The U.S. Treasury must sell literally trillions of dollars' worth of securities each year to cover the federal budget deficit and to refinance existing Treasury securities that have matured. When it sells securities, it generally auctions them to private middlemen like Goldman Sachs in multibillion-dollar chunks. But a tradition dates back to 1935 of selling government bonds to individuals that can't be sold on open markets, and thus don't change value according to market conditions because there is no market. To honor that tradition (as well as to provide a model for thrift), Uncle Sam still offers nonmarketable savings bonds in modest denominations.

Not so long ago, I wouldn't have recommended their purchase because there were equally safe, equally flexible ways to earn higher interest rates. But EE savings bonds are now sold on terms that are competitive with insured bank CDs, and they have some unique features that make them attractive. All U.S. savings bonds, like all securities issued by the U.S. Treasury, are backed by what lawyers call the full faith and credit of the U.S. government, and the interest is exempt from state (though not federal) income tax.

Paper EE Bonds
These are the savings bonds you remember from childhood—the beautifully engraved ones that you got from Granny on your birthday. They are sold in denominations of $50, $75, $100, $200, $1,000, $5,000, and $10,000. But, confusingly, the price of a new bond is just half the face value: a $50 bond goes for $25, a $500 bond goes for $250, and so forth. This dates back to the days when the interest rate was calculated to double the value of the bond at maturity (which made it

possible for Granny to look like a big spender by giving you a $100 bond that cost her just $50).

The interest rate is set at 85 percent of the rate paid on marketable Treasury securities with a five-year maturity that are sold in the big auctions. Interest is only paid when the bond is cashed in. The rate remains fixed for twenty years. But the Treasury guarantees that the bond will at least double in value in twenty years as it accumulates interest (an annual return of about 3.5 percent). After twenty years, the Treasury is free to adjust the interest rate to market conditions. Note, though, that EE bonds stop collecting any interest after thirty years.

Uncle Sam allows each individual to buy up to $5,000 worth of EE bonds ($10,000 face value for the paper version of the bonds) each year. That probably covers the needs of most people. But there is no way to switch large sums from other savings into EE bonds.

You can buy paper EE bonds from most banks (including many online banks). Or, if your employer is one of forty thousand signed up for the Payroll Savings Plan, you can buy them through paycheck deductions. Most banks will redeem paper EE bonds, crediting the proceeds to your account. Alternatively, you can redeem them through the mail. For details go to savingsbonds.gov.

This old-fashioned vehicle for personal savings stands up pretty well in a world of newfangled investments:

- True, they can't be redeemed for cash for one year, so they're not a suitable substitute for a NOW account or a money market fund. For the following four years, though, the redemption penalty is just three months' interest—matching most bank CDs. After five years, there are no more penalties.

- The interest rate is in the ballpark of what you'd expect from an insured CD. And you have the option of collecting returns at the original, fixed rate for at least twenty years.

- You don't pay state or local income tax on the interest, and federal tax is deferred until you redeem the bond. Among other things, that deferral may make it possible to time the tax liability to a year in which you are in a lower tax bracket.

- The interest on EE bonds isn't taxed at all if the proceeds are used for college expenses. There are some restrictions—in particular, the annual family income of the college attendee must be less than about $135,000 (that income ceiling is inching up each year along with inflation). But this can be a sweet deal.

Electronic EE Bonds

Virtually all federal securities have been converted to electronic form—imagine the problems in keeping track of paper representing close to $6 trillion worth of federal debt held outside the federal government.* While the government still issues paper versions of EE bonds in deference to tradition, Uncle Sam has worked hard to make it easy to buy EE bonds online, direct from the Treasury. The one minor difference: electronic EE bonds sell for their face value, and in any amount between $25 and the $5,000 maximum annual purchase. So if you want, you can buy a $38 EE bond (for $38).

---

* Another $5 trillion is owed by one federal agency to another. But that's a different story.

Buying electronic EEs is pretty simple. You open an account at TreasuryDirect, the Treasury's online center for individuals who want to purchase all manner of Treasury securities from the source. (Visit treasurydirect.gov and register at the secure TreasuryDirect Web site.) Then, following the site's instructions, you can transfer money electronically from any bank account.

Redeeming bonds is equally straightforward, provided, of course, that you've held them at least a year. TreasuryDirect will automatically forward the money to your bank account.

INFLATION-PROTECTED SECURITIES

You can't lose a penny on an insured bank CD or a EE U.S. savings bond. But the value of all those pennies you've socked away can and does erode as the cost of living rises. This is no small matter, especially for savings accumulated for retirement: just 2 percent inflation (well below the rate in 2008) cuts the purchasing power of a dollar by half in thirty-five years.

You can factor inflation into decisions about how much you need to save to meet your goals. But that doesn't change the reality that few long-term investments track inflation: if you buy an EE bond paying 3 percent interest, it will pay 3 percent next year and the next whether the inflation rate is 1 percent or 21 percent. Economists used to argue that stocks were a pretty good hedge against inflation because they represent shares in real things such as machines and buildings, but it hasn't always worked out that way.

So what's a conservative, inflation-wary investor to do?

Series I U.S. Savings Bonds

One answer is to buy a version of U.S. savings bonds with inflation protection built in. In some respects, they're just like
EE bonds. Series I bonds come in both paper and electronic
versions; the same $5,000 restriction on annual purchases by
an individual applies. You buy and sell them the same way,
too, through the same channels—banks, payroll savings, or
on a Treasury Web site. But the calculation of interest is very
different.

The interest rate paid on I bonds has two components: a
fixed rate set when the bond is issued, and an inflation adjustment calculated every six months from the government's
consumer price index. The math is a bit messy. But what
counts is that the bond's redemption value grows just enough
to offset inflation and to deliver a "real" (inflation-adjusted)
return equal to the fixed rate set the day you buy the bond.

On first glance,* the fixed-rate component offered may
seem shockingly low. In fact, the rate set for the six months
ending November 1, 2008, was 0.00 percent. That's right:
nothing, zip, nada. So all you can expect from I bonds sold
between May and November 2008 is that your investment
will hold its value after adjusting for inflation. Actually it's
worse: the "income" (that is, the inflation component of the
return) is still subject to federal taxes at redemption.

This isn't quite as unreasonable as it first appears. The
zero-percent rate was chosen by the Treasury based on the
after-inflation return you could get on comparable federally
insured investments (bank CDs) that don't have an inflation

If you care to look yourself, the table of the fixed rates offered in past
years can be viewed at treasurydirect.gov/indiv/research/indepth/
ibonds/res_ibonds_iratesandterms.htm.

adjustment built in. If there's something to be outraged about here, it's that Washington taxes the portion of interest that amounts to nothing more than inflation. A low-interest environment for borrowers is needed to get the economy moving again after the market crash, but this makes the job of saving for college or retirement that much more difficult.

Treasury Inflation-Protected Securities (TIPS)

Series I bonds are designed with small investors in mind. They come in small denominations (as little as $25) and are always worth at least what you paid for them. On the other hand, an individual can only buy $5,000 worth annually. And if you need to cash them in during the first year, you're out of luck.

TIPS, by contrast, are designed for investors with more money to plunk down and more knowledge about how markets for Treasury securities work. They are a little more complicated to buy and sell, the taxes on interest aren't deferred until bond maturity, and they can lose a (little) value if you need to sell them before maturity. But on the plus side, they generally get a higher return and are not subject to many of the restrictions imposed on buyers of Series I bonds.

TIPS are sold directly by the Treasury. Alternatively, you can buy them through regular securities brokers (for a small commission), or you can buy shares in a mutual fund that buys TIPS on behalf of its shareholders (see below). TIPS are sold in slices of $100, with effectively no ceiling on how much you can buy. The securities can be had with maturities of five, ten, and twenty years. But since they can be bought and sold on the open market (for a commission) whenever you like, you could rationally purchase them with the expectation of owning them for shorter periods.

The interest-protection feature is quite different for TIPS than for I bonds, though the result is identical. When TIPS are first sold by the Treasury, they pay interest determined by competitive bidding in an auction. Actually it's a bit more complicated: the Treasury sets the interest rate and that rate is effectively adjusted by the auction because bidders can offer more or less than the face value. But don't sweat it; you don't need to understand the details to invest wisely in TIPS.

That initial interest rate remains fixed for the full term of the bond and is paid to the owner every six months. What changes with inflation is the value of the principal. The Treasury adjusts the principal to match changes in the government's consumer price index. For example, if you bought a newly minted bond for $1,000 and over the next year consumer prices rose by 3 percent, the Treasury would raise the principal to $1,030. When the bond matures, the owner gets the principal back, fully adjusted for inflation.

Apart from being hard to calculate (though the Treasury-Direct Web site does offer a table to make it easier), this creates an oddity in taxation you won't like. The government considers the principal adjustment (as well as the interest) to be taxable income in the year the adjustment is made. So you are taxed on considerably more than the interest payment you actually receive. For example, if that bond we talked about earlier paid 2 percent interest ($20) and the principal adjustment was 3 percent ($30), you'd owe taxes on $50, even though you only got $20 interest in cash.

TIPS are marketable securities, meaning that you can sell (or buy) them through a broker in the blink of an eye. The catch is that the price you get in the free market could be lower (or higher) than what you paid. Thus the feature that makes TIPS more liquid than U.S. savings bonds—your ability to buy and sell them at any time—also makes their value more volatile.

Thoroughly confused? Don't take that to mean that you shouldn't buy TIPS. But it does mean you'll probably be more comfortable buying them indirectly, through shares in a mutual fund that does all the thinking for you.

To summarize, there are four ways to invest in TIPS:

Through TreasuryDirect. This Web site (treasurydirect.gov) makes it relatively convenient for individuals to buy virtually any Treasury security without paying a commission, and to hold it in electronic form in an account accessible online. To go this route, you transfer money from a checking account to your TreasuryDirect account before one of the six annual public auctions of TIPS. The Treasury then deducts the purchase price of your order (set by the public auction) from your account on the day of the auction and credits you with the securities. Interest payments are subsequently sent to your checking account.

When a TIPS matures, the Treasury deposits the cash in your checking account (or, if you ask politely, automatically buys a new TIPS with the proceeds). To sell a TIPS before it matures, you can order the Treasury to transfer the bond to a private securities broker.

Through a private securities broker. You can buy TIPS online at any time through a securities broker. The price you pay, though, on a "seasoned" security—one that has been around awhile—will be determined by the market. You'll also pay a (typically modest) commission to the broker. Interest payments on TIPS (as well as the principal value of TIPS kept to maturity) that are held by a broker are automatically credited to your brokerage account.

Through a mutual fund. A handful of investment companies sponsor mutual funds that invest exclusively in TIPS. Shares can be bought and sold (in most cases, without fees) from the sponsor's Web site or from most securities brokers (typically, for a small commission). The advantage of going the mutual fund route is that you never need to sweat the details, or even really understand the arcane terminology used in pricing TIPS. There are a few drawbacks, however. You'll pay ongoing management fees to the mutual fund sponsor, and (as with any marketable security) the share value will move around at bit.

Among the TIPS mutual funds, the Vanguard Inflation-Protected Securities Fund stands out because it charges low management fees. The minimum purchase is $3,000. For more information, visit vanguard.com or call 1-877-662-7447.

Through an exchange-traded fund. Exchange-traded funds are mutual funds whose shares are traded on stock exchanges rather than bought and sold through the sponsor. You buy ETFs from securities brokers as you would any stock listed on an exchange, paying the same commissions (set by the broker) that you would pay to buy any listed stock. In most cases, ETFs charge lower management fees than standard "open-ended" mutual funds. And in most cases, the explicit objective of an ETF is to track the average price of one class of security or another, rather than to trade to try to beat the averages. One other difference worth noting: open-ended funds buy and sell their shares at exactly the market value of the underlying securities. The price you pay for an ETF (and the price you can sell it for) generally tracks the underlying value, but there can be a bit of slippage because shares are traded on exchanges.

Two ETFs track TIPS. Both SPDR Barclays Capital TIPS and the iShares Lehman Treasury Inflation Protected Securities are now owned by Barclays Bank, and both assess low management fees. There isn't much difference between them, but I'd opt for the former—if only because of minor regulatory confusion in the latter in the wake of the collapse of Lehman Brothers. To learn more about Barclays Capital TIPS, visit the Web site ssgafunds.com/etf/fund/etf_detail_IPE.jsp.

OTHER U.S. TREASURY SECURITIES

Of the nearly $6 trillion in U.S. Treasury securities outstanding, the vast bulk are owned by big institutions—governments, pension funds, and other funds of various sorts. But Uncle Sam makes it fairly easy to buy Treasury securities directly, bypassing securities brokers and mutual funds that are also prepared to buy them on your behalf.

The terms of freshly minted Treasury securities run from a few days (!) to thirty years. Just to make it confusing, the ones with terms of one year or less are called Treasury *bills*, those with terms from two to five years are called Treasury *notes*, while those with longer terms are called Treasury *bonds*. Unlike the bonds and notes issued by corporations, state and local governments, and government-sponsored agencies such as the now-battered Fannie Mae, Treasury securities never have call provisions. That's a good thing: the issuer (Uncle Sam) can't demand them back if interest rates fall.

Treasury notes and bonds pay interest every six months. The money is automatically deposited to the checking account you designate or sent electronically to the securities broker that holds the securities. Since there are no paper versions of marketable Treasury securities, there are certainly no coupons to clip and cash. (If you don't know what I'm talking about, ask your grandfather about coupon-clippers.)

Treasury bills (aka T-bills) dispense with the idea of paying chunks of interest at specific dates. Instead, T-bills are sold at a discount from their face value. That discount—the difference between what you pay for a newly created T-bill and the redemption value at maturity—represents the interest. For example, you might buy a $1,000, one-year T-bill for $970. The extra $30 you get at redemption is the interest. That interest, incidentally, is liable to federal taxation, but exempt from state and local levies.

Payment of the promised interest and return of the principal are guaranteed by the U.S. government for all Treasury securities. But there is more than one dimension to safety in securities. It's important to distinguish between *credit risk*—the chance of default, which is zero in the case of Treasury securities—and *market risk*—the chance that you won't be able to sell the securities before they mature for as much as you paid.

Treasury securities that are many years from maturity can carry considerable market risk because changes in interest rates in the economy will affect their value in the market. Thus Treasury bonds (as opposed to T-bills and notes) should only be considered as part of an ultrasafe investment portfolio if you plan to keep them until they mature.

Buying through TreasuryDirect. It's simple to create an account on the TreasuryDirect Web site (treasurydirect.gov), make money available electronically from your regular checking account, and buy any quantity of Treasury securities in $100 multiples over the Internet after the public auction. Interest, as well as proceeds from maturing securities, is automatically deposited to your checking account or, on your instructions, used to purchase a new round of the same securities. The interest rate you get from TreasuryDirect is determined by the rate set by the public auction.

Buying through a securities broker. Virtually all brokers offer Treasury securities from new auctions, as well as through the ongoing "secondary" market for securities already issued. Unlike TreasuryDirect, however, brokers are free to charge (generally modest) fees and may require a minimum purchase much larger than the TreasuryDirect's $100. What's more, they may not offer an automatic repurchase plan when securities mature.

A real question with both direct purchases of marketable Treasury securities (other than TIPS) and purchases through brokers is whether it's worth the minor bother. This is particularly true for T-bills, since banks offer interest-bearing checking accounts (technically, NOW accounts) as well as short-term CDs that often pay higher interest, even when you factor in the advantage of not paying state and local taxes.

The primary consideration here, I think, is insurance. If you are temporarily parking, say, $500,000 in anticipation of buying a house or making a major investment, it probably makes sense to keep it in T-bills because that sum exceeds the maximum amount insured in any interest-bearing bank deposit. Otherwise, it's hard to see the advantage in the Treasury route.

FIXED INCOME ANNUITIES

Annuities are contracts that assure you a series of payments at specified dates in the future. The classic annuity contract designed to minimize the investor's risk is an old-fashioned "defined-benefit" pension plan from an employer, in which you get a monthly check in a fixed amount until you (and usually your spouse) die. The ultimate annuity, one could argue, is Social Security. It pays every month for as long as you live and adjusts the payout to the cost of living. Social Security is, of course, backed by the commitment of Congress to deliver on the deal.

Annuities sold to individuals by insurance companies can, in theory, be the answer to a lot of the worries of conservative investors. In the simplest form, they work like pension plans, guaranteeing a fixed monthly payment for life. Lots of other investments provide reliable periodic payments—think of a U.S. Treasury bond with a thirty-year term, which delivers interest every six months for thirty years, then returns the principal. But few investments other than annuities can guarantee that you won't outlive your savings, and few allow you to spend the principal along the way.

Using annuities to guarantee a predictable income in retirement has major problems, however. First, the idea of the annuity has strayed far from the simple pensionlike contract; with all the bells and whistles that sellers add, the typical annuity contract is hard to understand. Since no two annuity contracts are alike, it is also difficult to comparison shop. Second, annuities are traditionally sold the way life insurance is sold: an agent spends hours or days with the client, working as hard as possible to sell the deal that generates the fattest commissions. Few of us are immune to this sort of salesmanship, thus few of us are likely to opt for the objectively best deal.

Third, changes in the tax laws several decades ago changed the focus of annuities from relatively simple, pensionlike contracts to tax-sheltered savings accounts called deferred annuities that allow you to use the proceeds to buy a real annuity later on. The resulting contracts can look good on first glance, but almost always have drawbacks that make them less flexible and less rewarding than alternative, equally conservative investments.

Let's start by getting off the table those tax-sheltered savings accounts that morph into annuities. With a deferred annuity, you plunk down a wad of money, the money earns income either at a fixed, CD-like rate or at a return keyed to the insurance company's returns on a specified investment portfolio. Then, years down the road, you have the option of taking out the proceeds and paying the taxes on the earnings (which have been deferred), or trading the accumulated cash for an immediate fixed annuity that pays out like a pension. The sellers of deferred annuities generally stress the tax-sheltered savings rather than the annuity features because few buyers ever trade in their accounts for true annuities.

Still, what's wrong with the concept of a deferred annuity? The devil is in the details. First, deferred annuities are illiquid. The insurance company sponsor almost always penalizes withdrawals before the five- or six-year mark. The IRS exacts its own (10 percent) penalty if you withdraw any cash before you are 59½. Second, deferred annuities are expensive: the insurance company sponsor typically charges fat fees to "manage" the account.

More important, the gimmick that made deferred annuities so attractive when they were invented—the ability to defer taxes on investment income—has been overshadowed by tax-sheltered individual retirement accounts (IRAs) and employer-sponsored 401(k) retirement accounts. With these, you get a tax break on contributions to the account, still get to defer taxes on income earned within the account, and generally pay far smaller fees. The bottom line: don't even consider deferred annuities as a means of saving for retirement unless you've maxed out your contributions to your IRA and/or 401(k).

That still leaves "immediate" annuities, the classic annuity contract, to consider. On the plus side, they offer a certainty about retirement income that other investments can't match. On the minus side, the contracts are inflexible, and the returns to your investment are apt to be quite low because somebody has to pay the salesman for his considerable efforts.

An annuity is, in effect, a bet about when you'll die. Most of the people who buy annuities are healthy and expect to live a long time. The insurance companies understand this and set annuity payout terms accordingly. Thus annuities are generally a bad deal for people who don't expect to live as long as their contemporaries.

If you do value the pensionlike properties of annuities enough to invest in one, the trick is (a) to deal only with an insurance company that has the financial cojones to make good on its side of the bargain far into the future, and (b) to get the most for your money by shopping around.

The former task is relatively easy. Don't be entirely put off by the collapse of AIG, America's largest insurance company, in the financial meltdown. The companies that actually guarantee the annuity contracts are state-regulated subsidiaries of larger companies, and they are under government orders to behave far more conservatively with their reserves. Even AIG's annuity subsidiary is generally considered solid.

Note, too, that state insurance commissions maintain reserve funds to meet the obligations of insolvent insurance companies in their jurisdictions. State-by-state information about insurance regulation is available from individual state

Web sites. All of these sites are accessible through a site run by the National Association of Insurance Commissioners: naic.org/state_web_map.htm.

Another independent source on the quality of the insurance companies behind annuities is the credit rating agency A.M. Best, which, incidentally, came out of the mortgage-backed-securities ratings scandals unscathed. A.M. Best provides ratings information online at no charge, provided you fill out a "membership" form. Visit ambest.com for the particulars. When you go shopping for an annuity, consider only companies with the two highest rankings, A++ and A+.

As noted earlier, comparison shopping for immediate fixed annuities is difficult. But a few guidelines will help:

- Avoid annuities that charge up-front fees or "loads." In theory, they may be as good a deal as annuities that collect all of their fees annually. But loads are too often a sign that the insurer is relying heavily on its commission-based sales force, rather than the underlying quality of its financial products, to sell annuities.

- Keep it simple. Like new cars, annuities come with all sorts of optional extras—in particular, guarantees that some or all of the investment will be returned to the heirs if the annuity-holder dies young. But there's never a free lunch. Such bells and whistles make it (even more) difficult to compare annuities. Besides, it is practically impossible to assess the value of such features.

- Focus on insurers affiliated with investment firms that are generally inclined to compete for business on the cost of services rather than on the charm of their sales force (see below).

- After finding the annuity that pays the most, perform at least one reality check. Could you generate almost as much income from interest payments on, say, a newly issued U.S. Treasury bond and still have the principal left over after thirty years? If so, the annuity plainly isn't worth it.

There is no substitute for comparison shopping, but four companies are a good place to start because they have both strong financial ratings and reputations for treating consumers fairly:

TIAA-CREF
The primary business of this gigantic organization is to manage pensions (annuities) for college teachers. But it will sell annuities to anybody. Visit tiaa-cref.org.

Vanguard
The gold standard among full-service investment firms, known for low-fee financial products. The company sells immediate annuities through the Vanguard Lifetime Income Program. Visit vanguard.com or call the annuity line at 1-800-523-0352.

Fidelity
The chief competitor to Vanguard in the low-cost, full-service investment business. Visit fidelity.com or call 1-800-345-1388.

USAA
This company provides excellent financial services at good prices—but only to military personnel (active or retired) and

their families (including grown children). Visit usaa.com or call 1-800-531-8722.

REVERSE MORTGAGES

Mortgages are loans, not investments. Why are they included here? *Reverse* mortgages, like other mortgages, are loans against the equity in your house. But they have a place in discussions of safe investment strategies because they offer a way to generate a steady stream of cash in retirement without putting the owner of the house at risk of foreclosure. A reverse mortgage is hardly the right investment for every retired person with some equity in a house. Indeed, the costs of this financial product are so high that it should be seen as a last resort for healthy elderly who want to stay in their homes, but need more income to manage it.

With a regular mortgage, you borrow money using the house as collateral, which guarantees that the lender won't lose money if you stop making payments.* With a reverse mortgage, you also borrow against the value of the house. But the loan is structured so you never have to pay back a penny until you leave the house.

That seems like a good idea for people who need income more than they need to leave a house to their heirs. But there are multiple problems. First, the closing costs on reverse mortgages are exceptionally high—often more than $10,000 on what amounts to a loan of less than $200,000. Second, many elderly eventually need assisted living; when they leave

---

* As the current mortgage crisis all too vividly shows, some lenders haven't always been picky about the collateral.

the house, the reverse mortgage comes due and they end up with less (or nothing) when the house is sold to pay off the loan. Third, the terms of reverse mortgages can be difficult to understand, especially for the very old people who really need them. Not surprisingly, then, it has been a business rife with scams.

Oh, did I forget to mention the fourth reason that reverse mortgages are problematic? The amount of equity in the typical house has fallen sharply since 2006, reducing the sums available to borrow.

If you (or an elderly relative) are prepared to venture into the reverse-mortgage thicket:

- Stick with lenders offering mortgages under the federal government's Home Equity Conversion Mortgage program. These federally insured mortgages limit fees and proscribe unfair terms.

- Use the reverse mortgage calculator available free online from the National Reverse Mortgage Lenders Association. It spells out the costs of a standard reverse mortgage tailored to your needs and estimates how much cash you could get monthly. Visit revmort.com/nrmla/index.asp.

- If there is a reasonably high probability that the resident will leave the house within a few years, consider a conventional home equity line of credit as an alternative. These loans are better deals as long as you are prepared for the possibility that you could be forced to leave the house once the equity has been drawn down.

Three sources of unbiased information on reverse mortgages stand out:

The *U.S. Department of Housing and Urban Development* has lists of FHA-approved reverse mortgage lenders, as well as locally available mortgage counselors. Visit hud.gov/offices/hsg/sfh/hecm/hecm—df.cfm or call 1-800-569-4287.

The *American Association of Retired Persons* (AARP) offers basic information and person-to-person counseling on reverse mortgages. Visit aarp.org/money/revmort/ or call 1-202-434-6044.

The nonprofit *National Center for Home Equity Conversion* offers a detailed tutorial on reverse mortgages on its Web site. Visit reverse.org.

FOUR

A Toe in the Water

PRUDENT RISKS, HIGHER RETURNS

One understandable reaction to the Panic of 2008 is to retreat to investments that put you at little or no risk. That is not necessarily a bad idea for people, especially those who simply can't bear (or truly can't afford) to lose more money. You're probably one of them if you're already retired.

But if you do choose to go the no-worries route, remember where it will leave you. The return on riskless investments is currently barely higher than the rate of inflation. The return after you pay any taxes owed may even be less than zero because the government taxes income that does nothing more than offset the impact of inflation. If you are saving for your kids' college tuition and/or your retirement, you'll have to save that much more to reach your goals. If you are already retired, you'll have to hold down your expenses more than you probably anticipated to be certain you won't run out of money.

This chapter is for people who have probably been burned

by the market meltdown and are inclined to take fewer chances than they were back in the days of the booming housing market, yet are still prepared to bear some risk in return for the chance to realize better returns on their savings. The list of investments that fit this category could be quite long—trust the financial services industry to come up with products that fit every possible need, and then some. But, just as nobody watches all three hundred channels that come with the premium cable package, nobody can make good use of every respectable investment offering available. So for the sake of simplicity, I've kept my list relatively short.

STOCKS

In better times, the case for investing in the stock market was alluring. The shares of individual corporations go up and down, of course. And (I don't need to tell you now) so does the market as a whole. But over the long run, the return on investing in even a randomly chosen bundle of stocks has been strikingly high. Over the century ending in 2007, investments in American stocks averaged an annual return that was fully six percentage points higher than investments in risk-free Treasury bonds. Indeed, this "equity premium" has been so large that hundreds of technical articles have been written in an effort to explain how it could have happened.

The catch, from the perspective of an individual investor, is that the returns vary wildly from year to year. That variability holds even for decade-long periods. Looking at every ten-year period over the last century (1905 to 1915, 1906 to 1916, 1907 to 1917, and so forth) the equity premium has varied from less than 1 percent to 19 percent. Nobody who is truly allergic to risk can thus afford to invest in stocks. But no one who expects the future performance of stocks to more or less match their past performance can afford not to invest in stocks.

That said, what's the best way to participate? Forget the idea of buying individual stocks unless you know something the rest of us don't or simply enjoy the game of stock picking. Mutual funds that invest in many stocks are generally a better way to go, if only because they can offer a true free lunch through diversification—a free lunch in the sense that, on average, you can expect the same return from a bundle of stocks as with any single stock, but with lower risk of losing a lot of the value.

All stock mutual funds aren't equal, of course. Some have done amazingly well over fairly long periods; others have sunk like stones. But here's the remarkable news: hiring fancy (and well-paid) stock pickers to manage a fund rarely works. Roughly two stock mutual funds in three actually do worse than you could do alone by picking stocks randomly.

The obvious answer is to pick a fund that has done well in the past. Obvious—but wrong. Numerous studies have found that the past performance of a fund offers no clues to its future performance. So, as my grandmother never said, what's a body to do?

You could pick your own stocks by throwing darts at the newspaper stock listings. Or, more practically, you could buy mutual funds that don't try to beat the averages, simply buying all stocks in proportions that reflect the relative size of the companies. These are called index funds because all that their managers attempt to do is to match the collective performance of a large group of stocks. There's a stock index fund for every taste. Some, for example, track the stocks of a single industrial sector, such as health care or technology.

But if you're my kind of investor, you won't try to guess which industry group will do best. Instead, you'll buy them all. While there's an index fund—sometimes a dozen index funds—available for virtually every statistically sound stock index, I'd limit my picks to some of the following, which are distinguished by both breadth of coverage of the index and low management costs.

Fidelity 500 Spartan Index Fund
Accurately tracks the Standard & Poor's 500 stock index of large listed companies. Management fees are rock-bottom, just .10 percent annually. Visit fidelity.com or call 1-800-343-3548.

T. Rowe Price Total Equity Market Index
Tracks what is arguably the broadest index of U.S. stocks, Standard & Poor's Total Equity Market Index. The downside: a slightly higher management fee and a 2 percent fee for selling shares back to the fund in less than ninety days. Visit troweprice.com or call 1-800-225-5132.

Fidelity Spartan International Index Fund
A superbroad index of stocks of companies outside the United States. Tracks the Morgan Stanley Capital International Europe, Australasia, Far East Index. Visit fidelity.com or call 1-800-343-3548.

Vanguard Emerging Markets Stock Index Fund
This fund follows stocks in developing countries, tracking the MSCI Emerging Markets Index. As with most Vanguard funds, management costs are low. Visit vanguard.com or call 1-877-662-7447.

Exchange-traded funds (ETFs) comprise another way to invest cheaply in funds that track stock price indexes, as well as price indexes for dozens of other asset categories. These mutual funds trade on organized exchanges rather than being bought and sold from the fund sponsor. ETFs have taken off in recent years. And with some reason: they can be traded at low commissions through any securities broker, and the firms that sponsor them generally charge low management fees.

Are they preferable to regular "open-ended" mutual funds? Yes and no. The low costs are a big selling point. But keep this in mind: unlike regular funds, the price of ETFs that are not heavily traded may not precisely track the underlying value of the fund's assets. Here are a couple of stock-index ETFs that are fully competitive with open-ended funds:

SPDR DJ Wilshire Total Market ETF
The price of this security tracks the Wilshire 5000 index, arguably the broadest index of U.S. stocks. For information visit the sponsor's Web site, www.ssgafunds.com/etf/fund/etf_detail_TMW.jsp.

Vanguard Total Stock Market ETF
Tracks the MSCI U.S. Broad Market Index, which covers over 99 percent of the total investment in U.S. stocks. For information, visit vanguard.com.

iShares MSCI EAFE Small Cap Index Fund ETF
Tracks a global index of midsize companies. For information, visit http://us.ishares.com/product_info/fund/overview/SCZ.htm.

iShares S&P Listed Private Equity ETF

This rare bird tracks an index of private equity funds—funds that invest in assets not traded on exchanges. For information, visit http://uk.ishares.com/fund/fund_performance.do?fundId=157850.

TARGETED RETIREMENT FUNDS

Most investment analysts advise investors to change the level of risk of their portfolios as they grow older—if you lose most of your savings when you're thirty-five, you can hope to recoup, but at sixty-five you have neither the time nor energy to recover from the blow.

Investors can always make the necessary changes themselves, moving from more volatile growth stocks and long-term bonds to less volatile stocks and shorter-maturity bonds. Or they can ask a mutual fund to do it for them. Virtually every fund group has a set of target-date funds in which you choose the year in which you want to end up with a conservative portfolio suitable for retirement. The real question is whether the game is worth the candle.

The answer is maybe. Adding these funds to a retirement account gives you the option of setting-it-and-forgetting-it. You can always change your mind later. However, you need to understand fully what the fund's investment strategy is because you may be more or less conservative in outlook than the managers who run the funds. And you need to be careful that the fund doesn't sock you with higher-than-necessary management fees. These funds aren't particularly complicated to manage. But, too often, funds view investors who want somebody else to do their thinking as novices unlikely to keep track of costs.

These three targeted fund groups charge relatively low fees:

Vanguard Target Retirement Funds (2005 through 2050)
These funds invest in Vanguard index funds, changing the mix over time. Exceptionally low fees. Minimum investment $3,000, except for funds placed in Coverdale Education Savings Accounts (see 102). Visit vanguard.com or call 1-877-662-7447.

Fidelity Freedom Funds (2005–2050)
Similar to the Vanguard funds, but the management fees are considerably higher. Minimum investment $2,500. Visit fidelity.com or call 1-800-343-3548.

American Century Target Maturities Trusts
These funds hold only bonds, shortening the average maturity date over time. Medium-level fees. Minimum investment $2,500. Visit americancentury.com or call 1-800-345-2021.

TAXABLE BONDS

Bonds are loans—contractual agreements for me (the borrower) to pay you (the lender) X dollars every Y months for Z years, then return the principal. They come in all shapes and flavors. Some are backed by claims on specific income flows. Some can be converted to the stock of the company that sold the bond. Some (called principal participation notes) pay interest rates linked to the price of commodities such as oil. Some contain call provisions, giving the borrower the option to return the principal early—presumably because the borrower has found that an equivalent loan can be had on better terms.

Once a bond has been minted and sold, it can change in value for two fundamental reasons. First, people (that is, the market) may change their minds about the chances the borrower will be able to meet its obligations. This *credit risk* is generally reflected in the bond's credit rating from one of the three largest credit rating agencies (all of them, private companies) that analyze bonds: Standard & Poor's, Moody's, and Fitch.

The other source of variation in the market value of a bond is a bit harder to explain. Bonds pay interest at rates fixed in advance. If, months or years after the bond is issued, borrowers find they need to pay higher interest rates to raise money by selling bonds, the market price of existing bonds paying lower rates will fall. No one, after all, would willingly fork over $1,000 for an old bond paying, say, $50 a year (5 percent interest) when you could buy a newly created $1,000 bond paying $60 a year (6 percent interest).

What works going up, of course, also works going down. When interest rates fall, the value of existing bonds goes up.

The risk the value of a bond will rise/fall because interest rates have gone down/up is called *market risk*. All securities that pay a fixed return and can freely be bought and sold are subject to market risk—even bonds issued by the federal government that simply cannot default. But note that market risk is closely linked to the term of the bond. A bond that matures in ten years is more subject to market risk than a bond that matures in five years because the owner of the former must wait twice as long to get his principal back. And since investors generally don't like to bear market risk, the longer the term of the bond, the more interest the bond is likely to pay.*

Okay, seminar over. Which bonds, if any, should you buy? That depends on your willingness to trade risk for potential profit. The obvious choice for those unwilling to bear credit risk is U.S. Treasury bonds. But in periods of considerable economic uncertainty—such as now—investors tend to "overprice" credit risk—that is, they worry more than is justified about the prospects that bond issuers will default on their payments. That creates an opportunity for investors with cool heads and reasonably deep pockets to profit from "high-yield" bonds carrying less-than-excellent credit ratings.

Bonds issued by the federal government can be had in denominations as small as $100 from TreasuryDirect, the U.S. Treasury's Web site (see 57 for details). Those issued by corporations, U.S. government–sponsored agencies (remember Freddie Mac and Fannie Mae?), and foreign governments generally come with a face value of $1,000. But, with the possible exception of Treasury bonds, I would counsel purchasing bonds indirectly, through bond mutual funds.

Individual bonds may not be sufficiently liquid—that is, you could end up selling them for significantly less than their apparent market value if you needed to sell in a hurry. Bond funds, by contrast, guarantee liquidity, repurchasing shares in the mutual fund for their underlying value whenever you ask. Funds also give you the advantage of diversification, which is particularly important in the case of high-yield

---

* Occasionally, longer-term bonds pay less interest, not more. But as my teenage daughter would say, this fact is TMI.

bonds. By owning shares that represent slices of many bonds, you reduce the chances of big losses from the default of individual bonds.

That said, you have lots of choices among bond funds that charge low management fees. The ones below reflect my preference for funds that passively track financial indexes rather than trying to beat the averages. The exchange-traded funds listed here are largely interchangeable with the open-ended mutual funds. Minor advantage: no minimum investment. Minor disadvantage: the market price of ETFs diverge a bit from the value of the fund's underlying assets.

Long-Term Bond Funds
These funds carry diversified holdings of bonds with long maturities—typically fifteen to twenty years. They will pay relatively high interest, but the fund shares will fluctuate more in value because long-term bonds are more subject to market risk.

Vanguard Long-Term Bond Index Fund. Tracks the Lehman Long U.S. Government Bond/Credit Index. Minimum investment $3,000. Visit vanguard.com or call 1-877-662-7447.

Vanguard Long-Term Bond Fund Index ETF. Rock-bottom management fees. For information, visit vanguard.com.

Intermediate-Term Bond Funds
A popular category of bond funds because these funds limit market risk, though at some loss to the expected return.

Vanguard Intermediate-Term Bond Index Fund. Tracks the Lehman 5–10 Year U.S. Government/Credit Index. Minimum investment $3,000. Visit vanguard.com or call 1-877-662-7447.

Vanguard Intermediate-Term Bond Index Fund ETF. Same deal, ETF version. For information visit vanguard.com.

Short-Term Bond Funds
These funds subject owners to little market risk, but pay relatively low returns. This category of funds got a black eye when several were trapped by big losses in mortgage-backed securities. These two, though, bear little credit risk.

Vanguard Short-Term Bond Index Fund. Low management fees. Tracks Lehman 1–5 Year Government/Credit Bond Index. $3,000 minimum. Visit vanguard.com or call 1-877-662-7447.

Vanguard Short-Term Bond Index Fund ETF. As with all ETFs, buy through a securities broker rather than directly from the fund. For information, visit vanguard.com.

High-Yield Bond Funds
These funds have fallen out of favor as investors seek to come in from the cold. One other downside: high management fees. They're arguably worth a place, though, as part of a balanced, diversified portfolio.

T. Rowe Price High-Yield Fund. Among funds investing in risky bonds, this one seems to do relatively well in hard times. Minimum investment $2,500. Visit troweprice.com or call 1-800-416-2981.

iShares iBoxx $ High-Yield Corporate Bond ETF. Seeks to match the performance of iShares' own index of liquid high-yield bonds. A low-cost way to put a toe in the high-yield waters. For information, visit ishares.com.

Tax-Exempt (aka Municipal) Bonds

Interest on bonds issued by state and local governments, as well as government-chartered agencies (think public hospitals, housing authorities, etc.) is exempt from the federal income tax. States also waive their taxes on income from tax-exempts issued within their borders—but not on bonds issued in other states. That can make these bonds a decent investment for households in the 28 percent income tax brackets or higher (for a couple, that's an income after deductions exceeding $137,000 in 2009). But, as usual, there's no free lunch: tax-exempts typically pay lower interest rates that reflect their tax benefit to high-income investors. So unless you are in the 28 percent bracket or higher, don't bother to read further—you'll usually do better buying a taxable bond or CD with the same maturity and credit rating, and paying the taxes.

How safe are tax-exempt bonds? Glad you asked. Tax-exempts issued by state governments that are backed by claims against state tax revenues ("general obligation" bonds) are generally very safe. Bonds issued by public authorities that are secured by specific revenue streams (revenue bonds), by contrast, are only as safe as the revenue. Industrial development bonds, used to construct facilities for businesses, generally bring up the rear since they are no safer than the ability of the private tenants to pay their bills.

As with other bonds, the issuers of tax-exempts can pay to have one of the big three credit agencies rate their issues. The interest you can expect to get is closely tied to these ratings. That explains why thousands of issuers with less-than-excellent credit, ranging from smaller cities to industrial-development authorities, have purchased bond insurance from one of a half-dozen insurance companies that insure bonds.

There is some question, though, whether insurers could

make good on their promises in the event of a deep and prolonged recession. That's probably reason enough for conservative investors to think twice about buying any tax-exempts—particularly tax-exempts that don't qualify for the highest credit rating without the benefit of insurance.

Actually, there is more than one reason to be wary:

- Tax-exempt bonds don't belong in tax-deferred retirement accounts (IRAs, 401(k)s, Keogh plans). You'd be sacrificing income for no purpose.

- The costs of buying and selling tax-exempts are much higher than for government securities, so it makes little sense to trade them with any frequency.

- Individual issues are sold in $5,000 minimums. That's not much for anyone who is sufficiently affluent to belong in this market. But it does mean you'll need to make a big commitment to tax-exempt bonds in order to buy enough of them to diversify your portfolio.

- The market for tax-exempts is not particularly liquid and reacted especially badly during the credit crunch. For a while, the market was so jumpy that the State of California was unable to sell short-term securities at any reasonable price.

- All bonds in the category are exempt from regular federal taxation on interest. But some (never general-obligation bonds) are subject to the federal alternative minimum tax. Just about everybody with a high enough income to make good use of tax-exempt bonds falls in this category. So check carefully that the bonds you're buying are exempt from the AMT before plunking down a dime.

- Tax-exemption doesn't apply to capital gains. Any gain in value of a tax-exempt bond that is realized in a sale is subject to capital gains taxes.

- Brokers who specialize in tax-exempt bonds, like brokers who specialize in life insurance, spend a lot of effort wooing affluent customers. That's a bad sign because advertising and a sales force are expensive, and the cost is generally reflected in the fees (or the resale markup) associated with buying a bond.

In sum, this is a tough market to navigate well unless you've really boned up on the subject. That's why it really pays to buy tax-exempts through mutual funds—if you buy them at all. As with taxable bonds, there's a wide variety of types of tax-exempt funds to choose from:

Long-Term Funds
As with taxable bonds, tax-exempts with more distant maturities generally pay higher yields—and bear more market risk.
T. Rowe Price Summit Municipal Income Fund. Low management fees for this fund category. The drawback: $25,000 minimum investment. Visit troweprice.com or call 1-800-638-5660.

Intermediate-Term Funds
An average maturity of less than ten years implies, of course, somewhat lower yields and somewhat higher market risk.
Fidelity Intermediate Municipal Income Fund. Middling management fees. Minimum investment $10,000. Visit fidelity.com or call 1-800-343-3548.

High-Yield Funds

These funds specialize in uninsured bonds not backed by solid revenues. Expect higher volatility; hope for higher returns.

Vanguard High-Yield Tax Exempt Fund. This fund hedges its bets a bit by putting a good chunk of its money into better-quality issues. Low fees. Minimum investment $3,000. Visit vanguard.com or call 1-877-662-7447.

Exchange-Traded Funds

Like most other ETFs, these invest "passively," trying to match the average performance of a representative sample of securities rather than trying to beat it. The advantages: low management fees, no minimum investment. As with other ETFs, though, their market price can wander a bit from the value of the underlying securities.

iShares S&P National Municipal Bond Fund ETF. Tracks the Standard & Poor's National Municipal Bond Index. No high-yield (that is, low-quality credit) assets included in the mix. For information visit http://us.ishares.com/home.htm.

PowerShares Insured National Municipal Bond. Tracks the Merrill Lynch National Insured Long-Term Core Municipal Securities Index. Note the big difference here is that all the securities are privately insured. For information visit invesco-powershares.com/.

Single-State Funds

Tax-exempt bonds are almost always exempt from state and local taxes in the state that sold them, but states don't generally extend the courtesy to out-of-state bonds. For example, California residents pay no state taxes for bonds issued in California, but do pay taxes on bonds issued in New York or

Texas. That explains why literally hundreds of tax-exempt bond funds focus on single states. (Nobody, of course, would bother setting up funds from states that don't levy an income tax.)

Beware, though, of some drawbacks. Bonds from smaller states are thinly traded, so the market may become illiquid. That could both increase single-state funds' costs of operation and their losses in a credit crunch. Rather than list individual state funds, I'm providing information about mutual fund sponsors that maintain funds from many states.

T. Rowe Price. Maintains tax-exempt funds for California, Georgia, Maryland, New Jersey, New York, and Virginia. Visit troweprice.com or call 1-800-638-5660.

Fidelity. Maintains funds for Arizona, California, Connecticut, Maryland, Massachusetts, Michigan, Minnesota, New Jersey, New York, Ohio, and Pennsylvania. Visit fidelity.com or call 1-800-343-3548.

Vanguard. Offers funds for California, Florida, Massachusetts, New Jersey, New York, Ohio, and Pennsylvania. Visit vanguard.com or call 1-877-662-7447.

REAL ESTATE

I know: you've been there, done that—and would rather not do it again. But I'm not suggesting that you buy chance-of-a-lifetime empty lots in the middle of the Arizona desert or even sure-thing condos in the latest luxury high-rise in Ft. Lauderdale. Over long periods, real estate has often proved to be a good investment. Since it comprises tens of trillions of dollars in wealth in the United States, it probably belongs in the diversified portfolios of those who invest for the long term.

But what goes for stocks goes triple for real estate: picking your own, or placing your confidence in a fund manager to pick for you, is a bad idea. The closest thing you can do to buying it all is to buy shares in a mutual fund that tracks the value of all real estate investment trusts (or REITs, the technical name for exchange-traded funds that invest in real estate property).

Vanguard REIT Index Fund
Tracks the MSCI U.S. REIT Index. Low management fees. Visit vanguard.com or call 1-877-662-7447.

Northern Global Real Estate Index Fund
Tracks the FTSE EPRA/NAREIT Global Real Estate Index, which includes European and Asian REITs as well as ones in the United States. Visit northernfunds.com or call 1-800-595-9111.

Vanguard REIT Index ETF
Same deal as the Vanguard REIT Index Fund, but trades on the American Stock Exchange. For information visit vanguard.com.

FOREIGN CURRENCY

The very idea of investing in foreign currencies seems exotic and dangerous, an adventure best left to the professionals. But the ongoing integration of the global economy, along with the introduction of inexpensive ways to invest abroad, has radically altered the landscape. Much of what you buy is made in countries with other currencies, so the exchange rate between the dollar and those currencies now directly affects your living standard. Yet, oddly, many investors who are careful to hedge their bets in U.S. securities never think to diversify their portfolios into other major currencies.

There's an important distinction between investing in foreign stocks and investing in foreign currencies. Foreign stocks do change in value as the exchange rate of the dollar changes. But a whole host of other factors also affect foreign stock prices. By contrast, buying safe bonds with short maturities (thus not subject to much market risk) is a pure currency "play"—a bet that the foreign currency will rise in value against the dollar.

Is there a good reason to bet that the dollar will fall in value? I think so. The dollar is overvalued in the sense that, at the current exchange rate, foreigners buy far less from us than we do from them. So, at present, foreigners (or their governments) must inevitably amass vast quantities of dollars (nearly $800 billion last year). And when (not if) they get tired of trading their TVs and cars and oil for the chance to buy U.S. Treasury securities, the exchange value of the dollar will fall.

But even if you aren't as sure as I am that the dollar will eventually tank, it still makes sense to put some of your savings into securities denominated in other currencies. Think of it this way: by keeping all your assets in dollars even though so much of what you buy comes from Asia and Europe, you are effectively betting that the dollar will appreciate.

A decade ago, buying safe, fixed-income securities in other

currencies was not practical unless you had a lot of money to invest. Now, options abound.

Foreign Bond Funds

Lots of bond mutual funds buy securities in other countries. Most of them, though, are just looking for higher interest rates and don't want to risk changes in the value of their assets as exchange rates vary. Luckily for them, there are sophisticated (if not always cheap) ways to neutralize exchange risk. But a few funds deliberately expose their shareholders to the risk of changes in exchange rates—precisely what we want as a means to hedge against the decline of the dollar.

Oppenheimer International Bond Fund. This fund does just what you'd like it to, investing in high-quality bonds denominated in diverse foreign currencies. I have to grit my teeth to recommend it, however, because the fees are so large: first a 4.75 percent sales charge, then close to 1 percent in annual management fees. Buy it only if you plan to hold for several years, if you buy it at all. Visit oppenheimerfunds.com or call 1-888-470-0862.

American Century International Bond Fund. Much like the Oppenheimer fund; invests in a mix of bonds, mostly in Europe and Japan, with average maturities of about five years. Like Oppenheimer, it charges a 4.75 percent initial sales charge. The one exception: anyone who owned American Century mutual fund shares before September 28, 2007. Visit americancentury.com or call 1-888-345-2071.

Foreign-Currency-Linked Bank CDs

An online bank called the EverBank specializes in federally insured CDs with maturities up to twelve months that rise and fall in value with the exchange rate between the dollar and any of a dozen currencies. Don't worry about how they get the federal insurance—the whole thing is on the up-and-up. The only drawbacks: relatively low interest rates and a $10,000 minimum investment. Visit everbank.com or call 1-800-926-4922.

Foreign-Currency Exchange-Traded Funds

There seems to be an exchange-traded fund for every financial index these days, so why not some ETFs that track the exchange rate of the dollar with other currencies and pay a little interest, besides? Why not, indeed.

Sharp-eyed investors will note that some ETFs tracking exchange rates and other indexes are actually ETNs—exchange-traded notes. The difference is small, but not insignificant. ETNs are uninsured loans to banks, which give you a little interest plus a link between the value of the principal and a specific financial index. So ETNs should generate slightly higher returns than equivalent ETFs, but shareholders must live with the (small) risk that the bank will default on the loan. In the spirit of conservative investing, I'd generally opt for ETFs unless an ETN offers a unique investment opportunity.

The most popular way to invest in currency ETFs is one currency at a time—which leaves the question of which currencies to buy and in what proportion. If you spend a lot of time (and/or money) in another country—for example, if you regularly visit relatives in Canada—it probably makes sense to buy the relevant single-currency ETF. Otherwise, you may be better off with an ETF that buys a whole package of currencies.

PowerShares DB G10 Currency Harvest Fund

Tracks an index of ten major currencies that is maintained by Deutsche Bank, the giant German bank. High management fees for an ETF. Visit ivescopowershares.com or call 1-800-983-0903.

CurrencyShares ETFs

The investment company Rydex manages individual exchange-traded funds for euros, Japanese yen, British pounds, Swedish krona, Swiss francs, Canadian dollars, and Mexican pesos. Management fees aren't bad. The funds track exchange rates with the dollar quite closely and pay whatever interest they can earn in safe, short-term bonds in the currency. For information, visit currencyshares.com.

WisdomTree Dreyfus Currency Income ETFs

This brand of ETFs tracks a host of individual currencies—notably currencies of three emerging-market powerhouses, China, India, and Brazil. Visit wisdomtree.com.

Barclays GEMS Asia 8 ETN

This new exchange-traded note tracks an index of the Indonesian rupiah, the Indian rupee, the Philippine peso, the South Korean won, the Thai baht, the Malaysian ringgit, the Taiwanese dollar, and the Chinese yuan. Downside: high management fees, some credit risk. Best information source: etfconnect.com.

INFLATION/CRISIS PROTECTION INVESTMENTS

Gold

When push comes to shove, what's the most reliable way to store wealth? Billions of people would answer gold. You can't counterfeit the stuff—at least not well enough to fool a chemistry major. It is recognized as valuable everywhere from Manhattan to the smallest village in India. I think there's a lot wrong with the almost mystical faith some people place in gold. But gold can help diversify a portfolio; the market value of gold (and other precious metals) generally goes up when the value of other assets is going down.

First, do remember:

- The cost of buying and selling gold, especially in small quantities, is generally high.

- Gold pays no dividends and earns no interest. Quite the opposite: you have to pay to keep it safe, if you've got it in any quantity.

- The price is subject to a variety of unpredictable factors—among them, changes in the cost of mining gold, industrial demand, and the policies of the biggest producers, South Africa and Russia.

I could still imagine wanting to put away some gold for a rainy day—after all, the price went from less than $300 an ounce in 2001 to close to $1,000 early in 2008. While I can't enthusiastically recommend it to be a part of your savings, it's worth outlining the best (and worst) ways to buy and store gold.

Gold Coins

Umpteen Web sites advertise gold coins, from the American Eagle to the Canadian Maple Leaf to the South African Krugerrand. You'll probably pay a hefty markup on the underlying value of the gold content, though. And the shipping/insurance charges are nothing to sneeze at, either. My advice: fuggetaboutit.

Gold Bullion

You can buy little gold bars at the same Web sites, and generally for prices closer to the market value of the metal. If you go this route, make sure you've got a safe-deposit box to store them in.

Gold Certificates

Now we're getting somewhere, provided you are prepared to settle for a legal claim against gold sitting in a vault somewhere rather than the shiny metal in your own hands. One certificate program, run by the Perth Mint (a state-owned corporation in Western Australia), has the advantage of low costs and guarantees from a stable government. For information, contact one of the two authorized American dealers, Asset Strategies International (assetstrategies.com) or Euro Pacific Capital (www.europac.net).

Gold Exchange-Traded Fund

Surely the lowest-cost way to buy and store gold. The first gold ETF, the SPDR GoldTrust, has been wildly successful:

the fund's assets exceed $20 billion. The management fee is a hefty .40 percent. But the shares are extremely liquid, and the only costs of buying or selling them are the regular commissions charged by your regular broker. For information, visit spdrgoldshares.com.

Commodities

As with foreign currencies, investing in commodities— everything from oil to pork bellies—has long been seen as an arena for experts only. Indeed, there is a long, dreary history of amateur investors putting their life savings into commodities and losing it all in a week. But the idea here is to invest in commodities as a means of reducing risk, not as a way to get rich (or poor) quick.

Commodity prices exploded in the last decade, and we're not just talking about oil and gold. Copper quadrupled in price between 2003 and 2006; corn prices quadrupled between 2000 and the beginning of 2008. Meanwhile lumber prices have bounced around like a puppy on amphetamines. Commodity prices may or may not be on a long-term upward spiral—much depends on the pace of economic growth in emerging economies, including those of China, India, Russia, and Brazil. But there's widespread agreement that commodity prices have become more volatile—and that consumers will bear the brunt.

The conservative case for investing in commodities, then, is to hedge against inflation much the way large corporations use various financial products to hedge against rising interest rates or fuel prices. If the idea appeals, the best way to invest is through exchange-traded funds.

PowerShares DB Commodity Index Tracking Fund
This ETF tracks the Deutsche Bank Liquid Commodity index. For information, visit ivescopowershares.com.

PowerShares DB Energy Fund
This one focuses on energy alone. For information, visit ivescopowershares.com.

FIVE

Eyes on the Prize

INVESTING FOR COLLEGE,
RETIREMENT, HOUSING

In twenty-first-century America, there's no end to the lovely things money can buy. But for most of us, the highest priorities are down-to-earth: a nice house with a mortgage that will eventually be paid off . . . the chance to send the kids to college (maybe a private college) without loading them up with debt . . . enough left over for the good life in retirement.

The bad news is that most Americans aren't even close to saving enough to meet these goals—no surprise, really, when you stop to think that the average family's income has hardly grown in the last quarter century. The good news is that, if you're willing and able to set aside money, Uncle Sam is eager to help by sheltering the savings from taxes.

PETER PASSELL

COLLEGE SAVINGS

Coverdale Education Savings Accounts

If you know anybody who's ever heard of a Coverdale ESA, chances are you know a tax accountant. The Coverdale is one of the best-kept secrets in the tax laws. Once you get a sense of the benefits, however, you'll see why it's worth learning about.

Here's the deal. Anyone with an income of less than $95,000 ($190,000 for joint filers) may create and contribute the maximum to a Coverdale ESA for the benefit of any child under eighteen, and the account can be set up at virtually any bank or mutual fund. If your income exceeds the limit, you can make a contribution indirectly by giving it as a gift to the beneficiary, who then makes the qualifying contribution to his/her own account.

The maximum annual contribution is $2,000—not a lot, but contributing the max to a Coverdale doesn't prevent you from saving for college in other tax-advantaged ways (see below). The contribution is not deductible from your taxable income. But the income the money earns within the account is never taxed by the federal government if it is used to cover the beneficiary's school expenses—be they for elementary school, high school, college, or vocational school. Most states never tax the proceeds, either.

The cash accumulating in the Coverdale can be invested in virtually any security—no life insurance, please. But the options are typically limited by the institution that's serving as the Coverdale custodian.

Change your mind about custodians? No problemo. You can roll over the money from one account to another (for the same kid) without tax consequences once a year. Or you can just set up a second Coverdale somewhere else—there is no limit to the number of accounts with one child as beneficiary, as long as the total annual contributions don't exceed $2,000. This latter approach can be problematic, though: custodians are free to charge fees to maintain Coverdales, and you probably won't want to pay fees to multiple institutions.

So what happens to the money if little Jessie decides to become a beach bum in Baja instead of a psychology major at Berkeley? You have the option of changing the beneficiary to one of Jessie's siblings.

Money can be taken out of a Coverdale at any time. No tax is owed as long as it is used for the beneficiary's tuition, books, room, and board. But the earned portion of money withdrawn from the account (in contrast to the principal) is counted as part of the beneficiary's taxable income if spent in other ways—and the IRS adds a 10 percent penalty for good measure. Ditto for money that is not withdrawn by the time the beneficiary reaches age thirty.

Other noteworthy restrictions are:

- Once money is in the Coverdale account, you can't take it back—it must be used on behalf of the beneficiary.

- As the "responsible adult" designated in the account agreement, you have the discretion to maintain control of the funds until the beneficiary reaches age thirty, the point at which the account must be liquidated. Or you can transfer control to the beneficiary once he or she reaches age eighteen. But after control is transferred, the process can't be reversed.

- A grandparent may set up a Coverdale, but the designated responsible adult must be a parent or guardian.

And only the responsible adult can distribute funds or change the beneficiary.

- The assets in a Coverdale count as part of the parents' assets in figuring eligibility for federal tuition aid.

- The legal provision that qualifies distributions for K–12 schooling expenses expires at the end of 2010 and may or may not be renewed by Congress.

Is the Coverdale ESA right for you? The accounts are simple to set up, but less flexible than the 529 plan and the U.S. savings bond approaches discussed below. Moreover, the maximum contribution is small compared to the likely cost of a college education. But there's no either/or here: you can maintain a Coverdale along with other college savings plans that offer tax advantages.

Where to Open a Coverdale ESA

As noted above, most banks and mutual funds are happy to set up Coverdale accounts and to do the minimal paperwork needed to maintain them. What makes some custodian/sponsors better than others are the fees they charge and the range of securities they sell for the accounts. The ones listed here charge no fees and offer a broad range of financial products.

TIAA-CREF. The nonprofit mega-pension-fund manager for college teachers will manage your Coverdale. Permissible investments: any of the eighteen (no-sales-fee) mutual funds run by TIAA-CREF, which cover everything from stocks to bonds to real estate. For information, visit tiaa-cref.org.

Scottrade. A big securities broker that sells the full spectrum of financial products. Coverdale customers pay the regular (quite low) commission rates to trade securities. But you're welcome to pick from any of some thousand mutual funds and pay nothing at all for the transactions. Go to scottrade.com or call 1-800-619-SAVE.

TD Ameritrade. Same deal as Scottrade—low commissions on securities purchases, wide variety of mutual funds with no transactions charges. Visit tdameritrade.com or call 1-800-454-9272.

U.S. Savings Bonds

This approach to saving for college (or vocational school) has been around a lot longer than the Coverdale ESA, but it is hardly any better known. That's a shame because it involves less paperwork and is more flexible in many ways than the Coverdale.

Here's how it works. If you cash in U.S. savings bonds—either the plain-vanilla EE series or the inflation-protected I series—and use the proceeds for postsecondary education expenses for yourself, your spouse, or any dependent, you never pay the federal taxes you would otherwise owe on the accumulated interest. There is no limit to how much interest you can exclude from taxation as long as the money is used for qualified expenses.

You don't need to specify how you'll use the proceeds when you buy the savings bonds or when you cash them in. There is, however, an income restriction: to get the full benefit, your income must be less than about $105,000 (the figure is indexed to the consumer price index) for a couple filing jointly. And qualified expenditures are a bit more limited than with a Coverdale: no coverage for K–12 schooling, or for room and board at any school. Savings-bond interest is automatically reported to the IRS. So you'll need to file a form with your tax return (Form 8815) to claim the exclusion for education expenses.

For information about buying U.S. savings bonds, see chapter 3.

529 Plans

Created in 1996 and named for the section of the Internal Revenue Code that spells out the tax implications,* the 529 plan is the mother of all tax-advantaged college savings plans. Anyone can start and maintain one—there are no income restrictions. The sums you can realistically accumulate within the plans are large enough to cover the cost of four years at the most expensive private colleges. And the plans are loaded with options. The downside is that 529s vary widely from state to state; you've got to do a little research to make the right choices.

Start with the basics. As with Coverdale ESAs (and Roth IRAs, discussed in the retirement-plan section below) the money that goes into a 529 plan is after-tax income: contributions can't be deducted from your federal taxable income. And as with Coverdales, the earnings portion of the money accumulated in a 529 is never taxed, provided it is used for the named beneficiary's college or vocational-training expenses (but not K–12 expenses). Unlike with Coverdales, however, you have the option of taking the money back and paying the taxes owed (with a penalty).

You can change 529 plans without incurring tax liability

---

* Just to confuse things, the IRS (but nobody else) calls 529 plans "qualified tuition programs."

once a year. You can even roll over one 529 plan to a new plan with a different beneficiary, as long as he or she is a member of your immediate family.

The 529 plans are under the jurisdiction of individual states,* which either manage the plans themselves or farm out the work to private investment firms. You can invest directly in a state plan or do it indirectly, through an investment adviser. I don't recommend the latter path, however; advisers add a layer of management fees, maybe even up-front sales charges. The advice you'll get probably won't be worth the cost.

Most plans welcome accounts from residents of other states, though using an out-of-state plan may disqualify you for a deduction of contributions from your own state's income taxes. You can use the proceeds to send your dependent to a qualified educational institution virtually anywhere—even in foreign countries.

The states set the caps on total contributions to a 529 plan; most allow up to $250,000. Note, however, that contributions to plans are considered gifts to the beneficiary under federal law and are thus subject to taxation after the first $12,000 per year. This can be gotten around: you and your spouse can each give $12,000, tax-free. What's more, you can each make a five-year gift in advance, effectively making it possible for each parent to make a onetime contribution of $60,000 to a plan without incurring gift-tax liability. Take care, though: most states that permit you to deduct contributions from state income tax liability also limit the annual deduction to $5,000, or even less.

---

* The one (important) exception: the Independent 529 Plan, run by a consortium of private colleges.

By my count, eighteen states (AL, CO, FL, IL, KY, MA, MD, MI, MS, NV, OH, PA, SC, TN, TX, VA, WA, WV) offer an interesting alternative to accumulating savings in an IRA-style account. They give you the option of prepaying tuition (buying future education either by tuition credit or by year of enrollment) and, in some cases, let you prepay dorm costs, too. Typically, the offer is good for any public college or university within the state.

Is a state prepaid plan the way to go? That depends. First, it's problematic unless you're pretty sure your kid will want to go to school in that particular state. The plans all give you an option to get the money back and switch to a conventional 529 account. But typically, you'll pay a stiff penalty in terms of interest or dividend income forgone.

One prepaid plan, however, is far more flexible. The Independent 529 Plan, created by a consortium of close to three hundred private colleges, lets you prepay for any of them (you don't have to choose in advance). The list of eligible schools includes some truly elite ones: Amherst, Carnegie Mellon, Johns Hopkins, Middlebury, Princeton, Stanford, the University of Chicago, and Vanderbilt, to name just a few. Of course, your child still has to be admitted . . . Check the Web site for details: independent529plan.org.

One other issue here is whether prepaid plans are better deals in purely financial terms. They certainly reduce risk—both the risk that your investments in a regular 529 won't pan out well, and the risk that college tuition will escalate faster than you anticipated. So one way of looking at the deal is that it's like a CD that earns tax-exempt "interest" at the rate of inflation of college tuition. Since tuition inflation has been running far ahead of interest rates that can be earned on safe investments, prepaid tuition can be an excellent investment.

For maximum flexibility in where you spend the 529 money, you'll need the conventional sort of account in which contributions are invested in securities and the proceeds are used to pay the bills for any qualified institution. That leaves the issue of which among dozens of plans (many states offer multiple plans) is best for you.

The first questions to ask are (a) whether your state of residency has an income tax, and, if so, (b) whether contributions to the state's own 529 plans are deductible and (c) whether the state extends the same courtesy to contributions to out-of-state plans. If there is no tax advantage to adopting an in-state plan, it clearly pays to shop around. If there is a tax advantage—and, by my count, there is an advantage in thirty states (AK, AL, CO, CT, DC, GA, IA, ID, IL, IN, LA, MD, MI, MS, MT, NC, ND, NE, NM, NY, OH, OK, OR, RI, SC, UT, VA, VT, WI, WV)—you'll still need to comparison shop.

That's because tax liability is not the only issue. Plans vary enormously in the fees they charge and the flexibility they offer in investment choices. It may thus pay you to go out of state, even if it means losing the state-tax advantages. Indeed, sufficient money is at stake here that I suggest you purchase access to a Web site specializing in analysis of 529 plans: savingforcollege.com. One month of "premium" access to Saving for College costs $14.95 and allows detailed comparisons among plans.

In case you don't care to pay for a subscription, here's a list of five plans open to residents of all states that hold up well in comparisons.

College Savings Plan of Nebraska
Managed by the Union Bank and Trust of Nebraska and Kansas. Notable for low management fees and access to low-

cost index mutual funds run by Vanguard and Fidelity. Visit planforcollegenow.com.

Virginia College Savings Plan
Managed by a state authority. Low costs, and an option to invest in (among other things) bank CDs. Visit virginia529 .com.

T. Rowe Price College Savings Plan
Alaska-based. Managed, of course, by T. Rowe Price. Fairly low expenses, nice choice of investment options. Visit price529 .com.

Scholarshare Savings Plan
California-based. Managed by Fidelity. Midrange on management fees. Nice choice of low-cost Fidelity index mutual funds, and even a "social choice" fund. Visit scholarshare.com.

UPromise College Fund
Nevada-based. Vanguard manages the investments, giving you access to low-cost Vanguard index funds. Interesting twist: you can earn cash bonuses for your account by shopping at stores in the UPromise network. Visit uii.s.upromise.com.

SAVING FOR RETIREMENT

This is the big kahuna, the savings that could spell the difference later in life between Caribbean cruises and watching Caribbean cruises on the Travel Channel. Here again, there is a wide range of choices of ways for deferring—or even eliminating—taxes on savings.

Traditional Individual Retirement Accounts

The traditional IRA is the Internal Revenue Service's equivalent of basic black: it's suitable for almost any occasion. But although IRAs are sufficiently attractive and sufficiently flexible to have become the keystone to the American private pension system, it doesn't mean it's easy to figure out the rules.

An IRA account can be set up at any time. Contributions for a calendar year must be made by tax day (usually April 15) of the following year. So your contributions for 2009 must be made by April 15, 2010. No exceptions, please; an extension obtained for your tax filing date doesn't apply to IRA contributions.

If you are under the age of 70½, you can contribute up to $5,000 annually to a plain old IRA ($6,000, if you're over fifty) as long as the amount is less than your total earned income—and you don't have a retirement account through an employer. With couples filing jointly, each may make the maximum contribution to separate IRAs. After 2008, the $5,000/$6,000 limits rise with the rate of inflation.

Deductibility is another matter. While there's a logic to the policy—Uncle Sam is worried that high-income people will use IRAs primarily as a tax shelter—the rules might have been written by a lawyer from Charles Dickens's *Bleak House*.

Contributions within the limits above are fully deductible from your taxable wage and salary income, as long as you don't have a retirement plan at the office. If you do have another plan, the contributions are still deductible if you and/or your spouse have an income below specified limits. Those limits, as of 2008, are about $53,000 for a covered individual, about $85,000 if both spouses are covered by another retirement plan, and $159,000 for a couple with one person covered. Oh, and did I mention that contributions become partially deductible as you cross these income thresholds and are phased out entirely when your income exceeds the relevant threshold by $10,000?

If this level of detail is confusing, don't fret. The investment firm or bank that serves as the custodian for your IRA can keep you up-to-date. What you should really remember is that middle-income Americans can put away far more than most do (or most can afford) in IRAs and reap the tax deductions.

So what's the catch? The whole point of the IRA program is to encourage saving for retirement—and to discourage backsliding. So, you can't loan yourself money from your IRA— the transaction automatically invalidates the plan and makes you liable for taxes on the entire amount accumulated in the account. And if you choose to withdraw money before the age of 59½, you'll have to pay income taxes on the withdrawal, plus a 10 percent penalty tax.

There are exceptions. You can make penalty-free (but not tax-free) withdrawals if you become disabled or have high medical expenses. Congress has also decided to waive the penalty for money spent on education or, in some circumstances, the first $10,000 of the cost of a house. But I wouldn't casually chuck money into an IRA if you are likely to need it before your golden years.

Speaking of golden years, between the ages of 59½ and 70½ you may allow your IRA savings to accumulate (and continue to make contributions if you are working). Or you may withdraw as much as you like, paying income taxes on the distributions unless you had chosen to make nondeductible contributions in the past to your IRA. Note that you pay income taxes at full rates on any distribution: dividend and capital-gains tax preferences don't count.

After the age of 70½, Uncle Sam insists that you make at least a minimum withdrawal each year and, of course, to pay the income tax. The minimum is calculated according to the average life expectancy of people your age. (You won't have to make this calculation; the IRS supplies a table, or the institution that manages your IRA will make the calculation for you.)

So what should you invest the money in? Start with what you can't invest in under the IRS rules: collectibles, life insurance, precious metals (other than some gold coins issued by the U.S. Treasury). Nor can an IRA hold the debts or real property of your family members—you can't buy a house for the kids, even if you're willing to charge them rent or to service a mortgage.

It's legal to buy tax-exempt bonds with IRA money. But it wouldn't make any sense since no tax is collected on income earned within the IRA account, and all distributions are fully taxed at regular rates, no matter what the origin. Investments in which the profits are largely expected to be in the form of capital gains are problematic, too—capital-gains tax preferences don't apply to IRA distributions.

The commonsense approach is to weight your IRA investments conservatively because most people can ill afford to bear much investment risk once they've retired. Also, most risky investments generate a return (if any) in capital gains, rather than interest or dividends, and capital gains get far better tax treatment when they come from investments held outside retirement accounts. So if you choose to own of mix of low-risk and high-risk investments (and choose to save more than the maximum allowed in a tax-sheltered retirement account), it's better to keep the high-risk, capital-gains-likely investments on the outside.

How you want to invest IRA money should help to determine your choice of custodian for the IRA account. A bank is fine if all you want to buy are insured CDs. Remember, though, that CDs in an IRA are only insured to $250,000. To invest more than that and still be protected by government insurance, you'll need to maintain more than one IRA.

That's certainly legal: you can maintain as many IRA accounts as you like, as long as your total contributions don't exceed the maximum. But having multiple accounts is a minor hassle, and if the custodians charge maintenance fees, the costs of multiple accounts could add up.

It's probably better, then, to set up your IRA with a securities broker that charges little or nothing in fees and offers a wide range of investments (including insured bank CDs and index mutual funds) at low transaction costs.

How safe is keeping assets in a brokerage account? No one guarantees that investments in securities, other than bank CDs and (temporarily) money market funds, won't lose value in the marketplace. But a federal agency, the Securities Investor Protection Corporation (SIPC), insures brokerage accounts up to $500,000 (including a maximum of $100,000 in cash) against losses if the broker goes bankrupt, somehow loses your securities, or commits fraud.

That's more protection than you may imagine because only a small portion of your assets are really under the control of the broker. Once securities (including money market shares) are registered in your name, they are not commingled with the broker's own assets. They're yours, and the only way you can lose them is if the broker steals them or somehow manages to destroy all record of your ownership.

So what's at risk is generally limited and rarely exceeds the $500,000 SIPC maximum even in multimillion-dollar accounts. Nonetheless, to make all customers more comfortable and to attract the tiny minority whose assets at risk will sometimes exceed $500,000, many brokers buy extra account coverage (typically with no dollar limit) from private insurance companies. If this is important to you, check with the broker before plunking down your money.

Here are a few brokers (among the many) that (1) will serve as custodians of IRAs without charging administrative fees, (2) offer a wide range of safe securities including insured bank CDs, and (3) charge little to buy and sell securities. If you ever regret your choice of IRA custodian, it is simple (and incurs no tax liability) to roll over the account to another custodian.

Fidelity

The giant broker does virtually anything a broker can do. Wide range of low-cost index funds. You must deposit a minimum of $2,500 or agree to an automatic $200-a-month contribution (not a bad idea) to open an IRA. Visit fidelity.com or call 1-800-544-4774.

Vanguard

Not a lot to choose between Vanguard and Fidelity. Fine service, low transaction fees, and a wide selection of index funds. $3,000 minimum for a new account. Visit vanguard.com or call 1-877-662-7447.

TIAA-CREF

Another low-cost, consumer-oriented broker. Since nonprofit TIAA-CREF's main business is running college teachers' pension accounts, it offers easy ways to convert IRAs to immediate fixed annuities once you retire. Visit tiaa-cref.org.

ETrade
Big online broker, featuring the usual line of investment products at rock-bottom transaction fees. No minimum to start an IRA as long as you are willing to receive your account statements online. Visit us.etrade.com or call 1-800-387–2331.

Roth IRA

With a traditional IRA, contributions are deductible from current income as long as a bunch of rules are followed. With a Roth IRA, contributions are not deductible—that is, they come from after-tax income. With both sorts, the account owners aren't required to pay income taxes on earnings within the account. Contribution limits for a Roth are identical to those for a traditional IRA. Why, then, would anybody opt for a Roth?

Start with the big reason. All distributions from a traditional IRA are subject to the regular income tax, and with few exceptions distributions before the age of 59½ are also hit with a 10 percent penalty tax. With a Roth, however, once you pay income taxes on the contribution end, you're pretty much free and clear. Five years after a Roth has been opened, you may withdraw the principal without triggering taxes. Once you reach 59½, distributions of the earnings within the account are also exempt from federal tax.

What's more, a Roth IRA has no required distribution at

70½, or at any age. So accumulations in a Roth grow tax-free until you need the money.

Still, isn't it better to pay the taxes later rather than sooner? That depends upon your tax bracket now and the tax bracket you expect to be in when you withdraw the money. Most people start in fairly low tax brackets early in their working lives, hit their peak tax bracket in midlife when they are earning the most, then slip into a lower tax bracket when they retire. So the Roth looks like a winner for most twenty- and thirtysomethings, while the traditional IRA hits the sweet spot for older working contributors.

But it doesn't always work this way. People's taxable incomes follow varying arcs; equally important, they aren't entirely predictable. (My guess is that a lot of thirty-five-year-old investment bankers with seven-figure incomes in 2006 will have to settle for low-six-figure salaries for quite a while.) Moreover, tax rates could change. With huge and rapidly growing budget deficits forecast all the way to midcentury, the best bet is that we'll see tax hikes after the economy has come out of the current recession. And though I consider it highly unlikely, Congress could always change its mind about Roth IRAs and tax the proceeds.

The only folks who can make the Roth/non-Roth choice without hesitation are those with high incomes who already have retirement plans through work, yet want to save more for retirement through an IRA. They should opt for the Roth IRA since their contributions to traditional IRAs wouldn't be deductible anyway.

For the rest of us, I would counsel a compromise. There is no reason not to maintain both a Roth IRA and a traditional IRA. So one strategy is to contribute to a Roth IRA in years in which you are in the 15 percent tax bracket (in 2009, less than $33,950 adjusted gross income for singles, $67,900 for couples filing jointly) and to contribute to a traditional IRA in the fat years when the tax deduction is worth more.

Note, however, that not everyone qualifies to contribute to a Roth IRA. True, unlike traditional IRAs, Roth IRAs don't have an age limit for contributions. But there is an income limit for contributors. In 2008, only individuals with incomes less than $101,000 and couples with incomes less than $159,000 could make the maximum $5,000-per-person contribution. (Those over age fifty could add a $1,000 "catch-up" contribution.) After 2009, the maximum will be indexed to inflation.

Virtually every institution prepared to act as the custodian for a traditional IRA will do the same for a Roth IRA. Since securities brokers offer the broadest investment menus with low transaction fees, I would use one of the brokers mentioned above.

Note that, as with traditional IRAs, all sources of account income are effectively equal for purposes of taxation. With traditional IRAs, of course, withdrawals after the age of 59½ are taxed as ordinary income. With Roth IRAs, withdrawals aren't taxed at all. In both cases, then, the tax preferences accorded to capital gains and dividend income in other contexts are irrelevant, and there is no point in buying securities for IRAs with these preferences in mind.

Converting Other Retirement Accounts to Roth IRAs

The 1997 legislation that created Roth IRAs also made it possible to convert traditional IRAs into Roth IRAs. This served two purposes: encouraging people to save and—more important in political terms—generating federal revenue in the near term without raising tax rates.

When converting, IRA owners must pay all the taxes they deferred in making contributions. Presumably they wouldn't bother converting if they didn't have more to gain in reduced taxes down the road than they lost in taxes paid up front. Yet, by the convoluted logic of a law intended to force Congress to balance the budget, the legislators got credit for raising revenue immediately but paid no penalty for revenue lost far in the future.

In any event, Congress's opportunism may be your opportunity. Provided your income (as an individual) is less than $100,000, you can convert all or just a portion of a traditional IRA by paying the income tax. So, for example, if you have a traditional IRA with, say, $500,000 in assets, you can take $50,000 of it, pay income taxes on the $50,000 at your current tax rate, and transfer that money to a Roth IRA. You can do the same thing next year, and the next. In 2010, by the way, the rule restricting conversions to people with incomes below $100,000 will be lifted. Anybody (at any age) will have the option of converting.

But should you convert? Once again, the answer turns on expectations of future tax rates. The same factors discussed above that affect the choice between funding a traditional IRA or a Roth IRA should drive this decision. Since time is money in finance, it generally makes sense to delay taxation—implying that the traditional IRA is, more often than not, the better bet. But not always: if your tax bracket is lower now than it is likely to be when you retire and are obliged to take distributions from a traditional IRA, it may well make sense to convert. If, for example, you experience a dip in income and temporarily drop to a lower tax bracket, you can convert that year and enjoy tax-free IRA distributions later.

One other consideration looms here. Huge and growing budget deficits will almost certainly force Washington to raise taxes in the future. If you've converted your IRA, though, it won't be your problem.

SEP-IRA

Wage earners are tightly limited on their maximum tax-deductible contributions to IRAs. But those who are self-employed (or moonlight on their own) have a dandy way to put away as much as $46,000 in 2008, $48,000 in 2009, and $50,000 in 2010 by creating a "simplified employee pension" IRA. Note, however, that if you have employees, the rules require you to cover them, too, if they are over the age of twenty-one, have worked for you three of the previous five years, and made at least $500. But here, I assume that you are the only worker covered by your plan, and that the income is in the form of business profits.

Here's how it works. You set up an account at an investment institution (bank, broker, etc.) and contribute to the account by tax time of the following year. For example, the deadline for calendar year 2008 is April 15, 2009. The paperwork is pretty simple—a single form provided by the plan custodian—with no annual reporting requirement other than disclosing contributions on your regular income tax return. If you have a regular job as well as a business, you're still welcome to participate in your employer's pension plan.

In most respects, the SEP-IRA rules parallel those of a traditional IRA:

- Contributions are deductible from current taxable income.

- No loans from the account to you or anyone else are permitted.

- No mandatory contributions (if you're feeling poor or just have to take that cruise).

- Full tax liability, plus 10 percent penalty, for withdrawals before age 59½.

- Mandatory minimum withdrawals after age 70½, keyed to life expectancy.

- Can be converted whole, or in part, to a Roth IRA.

What's very different, though, is the calculation of maximum contributions. Trust the lawyers to make this confusing. The rules say something about contributing 25 percent of profits, but go on to explain that, by 25 percent, the law really means 20 percent. Wait, not quite, since self-employment contributions to Social Security have to be subtracted first . . .

It turns out that the maximum is somewhere between 18 and 19 percent of net profits from self-employment. The custodian of the account will be happy to make the actual calculation for you. Or you can use this calculator, courtesy of Fidelity Investments: http://personal.fidelity.com/products/retirement/getstart/newacc/sepiracalc.shtml.cvsr.

In any event, the maximum can be quite hefty. In 2008, for example, a self-employed consultant who earned $150,000 after expenses could contribute $28,333.

401(k) Plans

Named after a section of the federal tax code, 401(k) plans are "defined contribution" retirement plans sponsored by private employers that give employees considerable discretion to sock away part of their pay while deferring taxes. Congress has also given employers the discretion to set up Roth 401(k)s that are funded with after-tax earnings. Workers can contribute to either or both.

Employees of nonprofits may have access to similar 403(b) plans, while employees of state and local governments sometimes have access to roughly equivalent 457 Plans. Each kind differs from 401(k) plans in some ways, so don't assume that every word of the following description applies to them.

With 401(k)s, employees decide whether they want to contribute and, if they do, how much from each paycheck. The annual maximum is $15,500 in 2008 and $16,500 in 2009. Thereafter, the max will be indexed to inflation. Workers over the age of fifty can also make "catch-up" contributions—up to $5,500 extra in 2009. What's more, employers have broad discretion to sweeten the deal with matching contributions, and many do. But under no circumstance can the total employer-employee contribution exceed $46,900 in 2009.

To ensure that the 401(k) doesn't become just another perk to feather the bosses' nests, the amount that "highly paid" employees (those earning over $100,000) can contribute is constrained by the rate of participation of the lower-paid worker bees. To cynics, that explains why many companies try so hard to get employees to sign up, and why they make generous matching payments.

Most employers farm out the administration of their 401(k) plans to investment firms. These administrators typically decide—sometimes with input from employees—the range of investments available to contributors. Usually this includes a broad menu of mutual funds, which may charge substantial management fees. Check this carefully: in choosing administrators, employers may pay more attention to their own administrative costs (or their old-boy network of financial advisers) than to their employees' interests.

Many plans permit you to invest part of your contributions in the employer's stock, perhaps at a discount from market value. You may feel pressure, real or imagined, to buy company stock. Resist it if you can. Your financial future is inevitably tied closely to the fortunes of your employer, so it makes sense to diversify by investing 401(k) money somewhere else. (If you are afraid of not being seen as a team player, perhaps the memory of what happened to Enron employees' 401(k)s after the company went broke will stiffen your backbone.)

All things considered, 401(k)s are usually a terrific way to set aside substantial sums with the same tax advantages offered by IRAs. The withdrawal rules are relatively flexible— no need to take out cash at any age as long as you're working. The plans are "portable" in the sense that they can be rolled over to a new employer's 401(k) plan or into your own IRA. (However, the full amount of the employer's contribution may not be "vested"; some of it may go back to the employer if you quit.)

Consider, too, that contributors to 401(k)s—in contrast to contributors to IRAs—are usually given some discretion by the plan to borrow from the accounts. Such loans, however, cannot exceed 50 percent of the account value or $50,000, whichever is less. And unless the money is used to buy a house, the loans must be paid back within five years. Most plans also give you the option of making withdrawals in times of "hardship." Taxes must be paid on these distributions in the year they are taken, but the IRS won't assess a penalty tax as long as you meet a test for "heavy and immediate financial need." Plan administrators will usually help in figuring out whether you meet the test.

Keogh Plans

Keoghs are full-blown pension plans, primarily designed for small businesses but used by some self-employed individuals. They are complicated to set up, and the reporting requirements (to the Department of Labor) can be onerous. What's more, the benefits are generally similar to those of SEP-IRAs, which are a snap to administer. Indeed, many individuals with Keogh Plans have found that it makes a lot of sense to roll their assets into the much simpler SEP-IRAs. So why discuss Keoghs here?

One type of Keogh, the "defined benefit" Keogh, works like the defined-benefit plans that large employers used to give to their employees (a few still do). With a Keogh defined-benefit plan for an individual, you put aside tax-deferred dollars from your profits with the goal of funding an annuity that will pay a fixed monthly benefit for life once you retire. These plans are terribly complex—so complex that you need to hire a pension consultant to create one that passes muster with the government. Moreover, once you've committed to the rigid terms, they are equally complex to unravel.

Why bother? These plans give you a chance to put aside a far larger percentage of your income, deferring taxation until you start receiving the (fully taxable) annuity payouts. So, if you make several hundred thousand dollars a year in self-employment income and are willing to jump through some hoops, a defined-benefit Keogh may be right for you.

INVESTING IN A HOUSE

The wondrous days of no-money-down, we'll-start-worrying-about-the-payments-when-the-sheriff-shows-up mortgages are surely over. For the foreseeable future, it's going to be difficult to obtain any mortgage without a hefty down payment along with evidence that you'll be able to meet your obligations without selling your children into slavery.

But it's not all bad news. House prices are once again approaching rational levels in the postbubble market. Someday relatively soon, $800,000 mini-McMansions in Southern California may once again go for $400,000, while three-bedroom, two-and-a-half-bath ranch houses in most of the rest of the country may again be within reach of middle-income Americans. Once the housing market settles down, over the long run the value of your housing investment will probably grow.

What's more, the tax code will continue to look favorably on those who occupy their own houses. If you own, say, $400,000 in bank CDs, you have to cough up taxes every year on the interest. But if you own a house worth $400,000, the services you get from the dwelling (think of it as rent you pay to yourself) are tax-free. The law also gives you a free ride on any capital gain if you choose to sell—up to $250,000 for an individual and $500,000 for a couple filing jointly.

This is no place to outline strategies for investing in housing—they'd fill a book all on their own. But a couple of points that often escape mention are worth noting here:

- With some exceptions, mortgage interest is deductible from taxable income. That doesn't mean you should take out the largest mortgage possible. In fact, if you have money to spare for savings, the best ultrasafe investment you can probably make is to prepay mortgage principal.

- The money you can "take out" of a house with a home-equity loan is a personal loan using your house as the guarantee you'll pay it back. But isn't it free money? By spending it, aren't you just spending a portion of your savings? Yes, in the sense that you might be able to realize the same amount of money by selling the house. But no in a more important sense: the house delivers the same services as a dwelling whether the market value is $300,000 or $600,000. Unless you are prepared to trade down to lesser house, or to move to some place with cheaper housing, tapping the equity for anything but vital needs (medical care) or other sound investments (education) is a bad idea.

- You can prematurely take up to $10,000 from a retirement account to buy a house (if you haven't owned one in two years) without incurring penalties. There's no pot of gold here: you must still pay income taxes on the distribution. But this rule may give you the flexibility to stash more cash in a retirement account without worrying that you'll someday lack a down payment on that bargain house of a lifetime.

SIX

Keeping Up

Most of the analysis and advice in previous chapters should work for all seasons. But the world of investing is always changing. Moreover the pace of change is likely to accelerate as government policymakers push for reforms in the wake of the Panic of 2008, and the humbled financial community regains its taste for hunting and gathering.

Here, I offer a short list of Web sites that can keep you up-to-date, simplify the myriad calculations needed to make smart investment choices, and allow you to appraise the latest, greatest financial innovations soon (no doubt) to be touted by a rejuvenated Wall Street.

FINANCIAL NEWS YOU CAN REALLY USE

Bloomberg News (bloomberg.com)
The company that revolutionized the electronic dissemination of financial information (and provided New York with

PETER PASSELL

its mayor) has a wonderful flagship Web site. While it costs a lot of money to get online access to the full torrent of information generated by Bloomberg's reporters and computers, the more limited free version serves up more than enough to satisfy most investors' appetites.

The front page/home page provides:

- data, constantly refreshed, from every major (and most minor) financial markets.

- headlines of the latest economic, business, and finance-related news and, with a click, the stories by Bloomberg's own reporters.

- "editors' picks" of finance-related videos.

- Bloomberg radio feeds as well as nine (!) channels of Bloomberg television, live from Europe, Asia, and Latin America, as well as the United States.

- links to a wide selection of investment tools, including a Bloomberg toolbar that connects you to all the Bloomberg news feeds.

Google Finance (finance.google.com),
MSN Money (moneycentral.msn.com),
Yahoo! Finance (finance.yahoo.com)
There is not a lot to choose among the three free personal-finance portals from these three Internet powerhouses. They all provide comprehensive financial-market data, business and financial news, and lots of small-investor-oriented service features.

Of the three, though, I generally like the mix of features

(and the look) of Yahoo! Finance. It even includes a nice house-value estimator, as well as links for searching jobs, cars, and real estate. Google, which does so many things so well, seems to have cut a few corners on this one.

New York Times (nytimes.com)

If you haven't looked at the *New York Times* in the last decade, you may be startled by how much more accessible it has become. Better organization and better writing have made it a faster, more interesting read. While it can't match the *Financial Times* or the *Wall Street Journal* in depth of financial and business reporting, it's very good. Best yet, it's free. (The paper does, however, charge for some premium services, such as software that makes the downloaded online version look like the print version and offers full archive access.)

MarketWatch (marketwatch.com)

The *Wall Street Journal* is expensive (see below), but *MarketWatch*, a webzine covering financial news that is owned by the *Journal*'s parent company, is free. Don't expect quality quite up to the *WSJ*'s reportorial standards, but *MarketWatch* is a solid, accessible source of financial news and more.

PAYING TO PLAY

Wall Street Journal (wsj.com)

The online version of the great business-news newspaper is now also aiming to match the *New York Times* in other news areas. The *Wall Street Journal* offers the best reporting in financial news, period. It makes full use of the Web format to present the news in ways that make it a faster, more-easily-targeted read than the print version. Moreover, the site provides access to the newspaper's archives.

The big catch: the *Journal* charges serious money for access—any access—to the site. The "rack" rate is $120 a year, but they usually run specials at $50 for new customers.

Financial Times (ft.com)

The *Financial Times* (*FT*) is the other great business-news newspaper. Better than the *WSJ* on European business and finance, but certainly not as inviting to read as the *WSJ*. You can read the front page and up to four articles free per month. Otherwise you gotta pay $100 a year.

Economist (economist.com)

The online version of the incomparable world newsweekly. The long "explainer" pieces on economics and finance are lucid and accessible to nonprofessionals. One cool feature is the podcast, an audio version of the entire issue that is broken into a dozen sections in case you don't want it all. Great for commuting or working out at the gym. Subscribers get it free.

Speaking of subscribing, the online version costs $80 a year, or you can get print, audio, and Web for about $120—a lot, unless you use it as the weekly alternative to a high-end daily newspaper.

INVESTING 101

The Motley Fool (fool.com)

One of the first personal-finance Web sites, and still pretty good. Specializes in teaching the basics in chatty, jargon-free prose. The advertising on the site is annoyingly dense, though. The Motley Fool offers a lot of content you have to pay for—columns of picking stocks, etc. I'd stick with the free stuff.

Kiplinger (kiplinger.com)

Kiplinger magazine has long been a down-to-earth source of information and advice for small investors. The free Web site, which the owners use to funnel business toward a variety of Kiplinger's subscription-based newsletters, offers most of what the magazine does well—explaining basics, warning about common investor errors, and rating mutual funds.

Investopedia (investopedia.com)

A really terrific (and free) financial-education Web site, with tutorials aimed at both beginners and experienced investors. Has a nice Q&A section, in which readers are invited to participate. Includes the Stock Simulator, an online game in which you make fantasy investments (starting with an imaginary $100,000) and compete with other game players.

Investor Words (investorwords.com)

A frequently updated online glossary of financial terms, now covering six thousand of them. Distinguished by its efforts not to use jargon in explaining jargon. Access is free.

Forbes (forbes.com)

This investor-oriented newsmagazine is consistently interesting and well written. *Forbes*'s ratings of mutual funds are among the most thoughtful, though I think most investors are better off sticking with index funds. It's always fun to read the rankings of the Forbes 400 billionaires. The site is free, but cluttered with ads.

Wikipedia (wikipedia.org)
If you already use Wikipedia for almost everything, why not investment information? Indeed. While there is some variability in the quality of the entries about finance, most are excellent. I found no errors—which is a whole lot better than many commercial Web sites dedicated to the subject.

INVESTMENT, GRADUATE-SCHOOL EDITION

SeekingAlpha (seekingalpha.com)
A free site that aggregates financial opinion blogs as well as offering its own content on investing. Tons of stuff, most of it smart and interesting. I'm particularly struck by the quality of the analysis of exchange-traded funds, one of my favorite ways to invest.

RGE Monitor (rgemonitor.com)
Nomriel Roubini teaches economics at New York University. He runs the RGE Monitor, a Web site offering his wise and deeply pessimistic perspective on global economics and finance. RGE Monitor was far ahead of the curve on the subprime crisis, and far ahead in analyzing what to do about the meltdown. Some of the Web site material is free. The rest is expensive.

NUMBERS, PLEASE

Dinkytown (dinkytown.net)
A terrible name for a terrific site. Here, you'll find some three hundred interactive calculators, available for free use. Want to

compare traditional and Roth IRAs? Just punch in the numbers. Or how much you'll have to put away for the kids' college tuition? The calculator is here.

Bankrate (bankrate.com)

A one-stop service for finding the highest-paying CDs, money market funds, etc. It even helps you estimate your FICO credit score. It's free, though once again you'll have to wade through ads to get where you want to go.

ESPlanner (esplanner.com)

Offers the most sophisticated calculator available for planning how much you need to save for retirement. Yes, most retail investment firms such as Vanguard and Fidelity offer conclusions based on your answers to online questionnaires. But this downloadable software designed by economists at Boston University does it right, even calculating the odds that market volatility will defeat you. Expensive ($150) and time-consuming to use, but probably worth it.

FINANCIAL COLUMNISTS
ALWAYS WORTH READING

Joe Nocera

Sophisticated analysis with the common touch. Nocera has been terrific during the financial crisis. Read him on Saturdays in the *New York Times* (nytimes.com).

Floyd Norris

This guy's been writing about Wall Street forever, but just keeps getting better at it. He specializes in ferreting out the slimy side of finance. Read him weekly (sometimes far more often) in the *New York Times* (nytimes.com).

Jeremy Siegel
A controversial scholar at the Wharton School, Siegel is an economist with strong opinions about investing—most of which are at odds with the academic side of finance. Read his contrarian column in kiplingers.com.

Ben Stein
This, of course, is the entertainer and movie actor Ben Stein. But his father was a famous economist (Herb Stein), and Ben has been writing droll, populist pieces about finance and economics for decades. Check out his column at Yahoo! Finance (finance.yahoo.com).

Jim Stewart
A former corporate lawyer and former *Wall Street Journal* editor, Stewart won a Pulitzer Prize in the 1980s for his analysis of Wall Street's shady doings. Now he writes a smart, readable weekly column on investing, to be found (appropriately) at smartmoney.com.

CALLING THE COPS

Securities and Exchange Commission (sec.gov)
The SEC has broad responsibilities in regulating Wall Street—responsibilities, alas, that it has not always taken seriously enough. The SEC Web site does, however, have a number of features that could help protect you from the villains. There,

you can check the records of brokers and investment advisers, file complaints, and tip off the agency about lawbreakers.

Financial Industry Regulatory Authority (finra.org)

FINRA was created by the financial services industry to police itself—and, of course, to keep federal and state regulators off its back. The Web site is the place to go to read about how to protect yourself from the latest industry scams, and it has a database of brokers who've done bad. FINRA also employs an ombudsman with the job of fielding public complaints, whom you can contact through the site.

Federal Deposit Insurance Corporation (fdic.org)

The FDIC is the federal agency that insures bank deposits. The Web site includes a "finder" that tells you whether your financial institution really is a member of FDIC, as well as EDIE, a calculator that can tell you whether all your deposits at a bank are insured.

National Association of Insurance Commissioners (naic.org)

This is the organization of state insurance commissioners, who, among other things, are in charge of policing the companies that sell annuities. You can order a free consumer guide to annuities on the Web site, and you can search a database offering key information about individual insurance companies.

Where to Find . . .

Printed in the United States
By Bookmasters